The Girl in the Tent

Memoir from the Road

Nancy DeYoung

D0731696

The Girl in the Tent: Memoir from the Road
By Nancy DeYoung

Cover Art—Robin Adams
Drawings—Alexandria Z Noble, Robin Adams

Please note that this book reflects only the personal experiences and views of the author. The information contained herein is for general purposes only. The author and publisher accept no responsibility for how the reader interprets or uses this information.

ISBN   978-0-9844103-0-9 paperback
ISBN   978-0-9844103-1-6 e-book

Printed in the United States of America

Contents

Introduction

Living in a recreational vehicle and traveling with my friends had long been a dream. In the 1990s, we talked about caravanning and *circling the wagons* at the end of the day. This talk never became a reality for us as a group.

I, however, experienced this lifestyle for almost a year, and it wasn't quite as we imagined. The reality was I had a tent, not an RV. I traveled alone and my only community was waiting at day's end when I pulled into the campground. They weren't people I knew, but these campers became my family and support group, even if it was just for a few days or weeks.

As I traveled, I learned there are many reasons people are choosing to live on the road. Younger people are making different choices than their parents and grandparents, whose primary goals were keeping their jobs and getting their houses paid off in thirty years so they could afford a trip to Europe.

Twenty- and thirty-year-olds are not waiting for retirement. They want to live life on their terms now and not wait until they are seventy years old. These young people are choosing freedom from high house payments, mundane jobs, and the responsibility of taking care of *stuff*. They have fewer possessions and are creating simpler lives that allow them to have their desired experiences while they are young. One advantage for this age group is many have jobs they can do remotely.

Another group I encountered was comprised of folks who have enough money to buy expensive rigs with all the comforts of home. These snowbirds winter in the southern areas and summer at their full-time residences, which are usually in a colder, northern climate. They did not seem to socialize with those who have smaller, less impressive rolling homes, and certainly not with someone in a tent.

Some people are not living on the road out of choice; they cannot afford a permanent home. Perhaps they have had large medical bills or made poor investments that have taken their retirement savings. They use what money they have to purchase a trailer or motorhome. They go where the weather suits them because it is cheaper and more comfortable not to deal with the elements. This is primarily the group that is trying to make a living by harvesting beets, cleaning toilets at the campgrounds, or working in warehouses during the holidays.

This sounded like a harsh way of life, and I asked myself what I would do. I am not a full-time nomad and have not had the challenge of finding work, but if I did, I would follow the lead of people who have built mobile businesses. They have customers in the places where they travel doing carpentry, teaching classes and workshops, and providing products or services.

Most of the people I met and interacted with were middle-aged or retired and lived on the road because they enjoy the nomadic lifestyle. They had modest RVs and campers and were the friendliest group I encountered. They were happy, helpful people who had nicknames for each other. There was *Minnesota Mike, Campground Joe, Tamale Man,* and *I was The Girl in the Tent.*

There are many reasons for being a nomad, and it is well to note that the number of people living this lifestyle is increasing each year and is expected to continue upward growth.

Is this way of life something that would be fun for you? This is the question you must answer for yourself; no one can tell you. I loved my time on the road, but I also knew this was not a long-term situation because I like having a home waiting for me. Until you know without a doubt that you are suited to living a nomad's life, don't put yourself in a position where you can't go back to a life closer to what you had. If you do, you may end up feeling trapped and come to resent your new life. Try the migrant life for a while before you make it permanent.

There is great joy and growth in spending time traveling and the nights under the stars, whether it is in a tent or a camper. There are challenges to be sure, but no matter who we are or where we live, there are always challenges. The questions become, what are the trade-offs, and which set of experiences do you prefer?

The idea for this book was born while I was journal writing after my extended time on the road. I was thinking about people who are trading their *sticks-and-*

bricks homes for the nomadic lifestyle of the full-time RVer. Many live a simple life, working when they need or want, and traveling where they want. To the free spirit, it can be a dream life of freedom, but it may not be for everyone.

The nine months I spent traveling triggered memories of the other experiences I had while camping. Although some of these accounts go back many years, they came to mind as fresh as if they were yesterday. I hope the experiences I have chronicled in *The Girl in the Tent* inform, inspire, and entertain you.

Story 1
The Plan

Today I fell on the ice. I went down hard. Annie gave me her hand, but I still couldn't get up. Michael stepped in, and with his help, they got me into her car. Annie had driven the 50 miles to the animal sanctuary, so we only had one vehicle; I was grateful I did not have to drive home. Annie took me directly to my bodyworker, and after fifteen minutes on his table, I could hobble to the car. When I got home, I collapsed, knowing it would be a while before I could walk pain-free. (December 13, 2018, Journal entry)

As I lay in bed, I thought about winter. The week before the fall, I was at Stephanie's house and couldn't get back up her driveway because of the snow. Her kids optimistically tried pushing my car up the incline, but no-go. Stephanie tried using her four-wheel-drive vehicle, but my car was stubborn, and all that did was scratch the paint on my bumper. It was no use; I needed a tow truck. It was time to make changes if these were indicators of what winter would bring.

Winter was just beginning and already I was tired of its inconveniences. I had had enough! I needed to make changes, but what? While watching the snow fall outside my window, I curled up under my warm, fuzzy blanket to ponder options for escaping another northern blast.

I loved my home and friends. My art was selling. It all seemed perfect, but despite the life I had, if I was to avoid another encounter with winter, I had to move south. Was I ready to make the hard choices I knew were required in exchange for living in a milder climate? The answer was "yes." The next question was, "Where?"

Since I have always loved Santa Fe, New Mexico, and its winters are shorter and milder than in South Dakota, it seemed like a good place to begin my search. Armed with a mug of hot chocolate, pen, and paper, I explored websites looking for affordable apartments in the Santa Fe area. As I suspected, the rents were even higher than when I lived there before. But not to be discouraged, I went through the ads anyway.

An apartment in Ajo, Arizona, came up in my search. It was in the old Curley High School that had been renovated into artist apartments. Everyone who lived at Curley was an artist in some form or fashion, and I would surely meet people like myself who worked with wood or dimensional art. This sounded perfect. I quickly sent in my application and didn't have to wait long for a response. A week later, Vicky called saying they accepted my application and were expecting a vacancy at the end of January. This was ideal timing, as I had obligations in South Dakota that would be completed in January, and after that, I was free to leave.

Ajo is not a destination location, but a town you drive through on your way to somewhere else. Many tourists pass through this small gem in the Sonoran Desert on their way to Puerto Penasco, Mexico, also known as Rocky Point. Ajo was once a booming copper mining town, but when the mine closed, many people moved away.

Buildings stood empty and disintegrating until some visionaries from the International Sonoran Desert Alliance (ISDA) began reinventing the town. The Plaza, the heart of the village, was brought back to life first. Then the grade school became a conference center, complete with guest rooms and an organic garden. The next project was turning the empty and neglected Curley High School into artist apartments; this was where my new home was to be.

I had been to Ajo two years prior while touring the Southwest. Although it is a tiny town, I remembered it because I had stopped to take photos of the murals that lined the walls in the alley. They weren't the graffiti I had seen in other cities; they were art with messages.

According to the plan, I completed my commitments in South Dakota by the end of January. I had rented a storage unit and each day I took boxes and small items to the unit. On this day, with the help of movers, I put the last of my things into storage. I left town that same day to avoid the snowstorm predicted for the next day. It was time for the adventure to begin, and unbeknownst to me, life would gestate for nine months before it birthed into the outcome.

With my car packed to the roof with everything I would need for an unknown amount of time, I drove the back roads through South Dakota and Wyoming to

Interstate 25. I have always enjoyed driving the open roads across the prairie where few cars travel. There are only enough towns to provide hotels, food, gas stations, and usually a mechanic if needed.

It doesn't seem there is much to see driving across these miles and miles of prairie, but if you look with an artist's eye, you realize it is not just barren land. The variety of grasses turns the fields into an array of colors. Mountains create a backdrop of mystery and majesty. The grazing cows and horses, lone cottonwood trees, vast forever-changing sky, spinning windmills, dry creek beds, and snow fences all adorn the expansive vistas.

A Wintery Scene in Wyoming

One of my favorite pastimes is counting cars on the seemingly endless stream of coal trains. I quickly lose track of the number, but I found they are over a mile long and often have four engines. There may be 50-70 trains per day through this area. They pass by, one after another, as they head east from the Wyoming open-pit coal mines. Traveling in the opposite direction are the empty trains heading back to the coal fields for a refill.

I often drive with my window down, so I can hear the meadowlarks and smell the sweet scent of the plant life, but this was January and there were no meadowlarks, only wind, and freezing temperatures. I shivered as I thought of the blowing snow I was missing by leaving a day early.

Many of my trips take much longer than my GPS says they should because I'm not usually a destination driver; I stop to see family and friends, take pictures, and explore things along the way. This trip would be more direct, with only a few brief breaks, because I was excited to see my new home.

My first stop was in Boulder to visit my dear friend, Peggy. I often spent the night with her and her husband as I travel through, but this time, I was on a schedule, as I had an appointment to see the apartment in Ajo. I also wanted to pause in Santa Fe the following day long enough for brunch with my friend Paula. Since it is a six-hour drive from Denver to Santa Fe, I would have to leave Denver at o'dark thirty to make that connection if I stayed overnight. Leaving then was not an option, so the idea was to just have tea with Peggy and continue south yet that day.

I have driven through Denver many times and I have learned that rush hour is something to avoid at all cost, so I timed my escape after the evening's big rush.

It's not just the Denver metro area to consider, but also the drive from there to Colorado Springs. That 70-mile corridor of Interstate 25 is always challenging, and the ongoing road construction further complicates travel, so it is best to do it when there is less traffic.

After a tense drive through the construction where lanes are narrow and serpentine left and right, the pavement is broken, speed limits are variable, and big rigs plentiful, I finally reached Pueblo, Colorado. I took a deep breath and relaxed.

I pulled off the interstate to get fuel for the car and a Dairy Queen Buster Bar for me. Then I continued south as far as Raton, New Mexico, where I stopped for the night. It had been a long day, and stopping there left me with only a three-hour drive the next day. Even if I stopped to watch the sunrise, I would still have plenty of time to get to Santa Fe for my scheduled engagement.

Paula was waiting at the restaurant when I arrived. After a quick brunch and a hug from my longtime friend, I got back in the car to continue the 450-mile drive to Benson, Arizona. The drive passed uneventfully.

When I reached Benson, I got a hotel room but didn't unload the car, as I wanted to explore Tombstone yet that day. The desert twilight is always stunning and would make the perfect backdrop for photos.

Tombstone, Arizona, is an old western town where many cowboy movies have been filmed. It is about 35 miles from the U.S. border with Mexico. Following my plan to visit that day, I drove south from St.

David. As I did, I encountered many Border Patrol officers in their shiny white SUVs.

A few miles north of Tombstone, I noticed cars were returning to St. David; the road appeared to be closed. As we waited in line to reach the officers who had set up the roadblock, two ambulances with sirens screaming came from the opposite direction. When I got to the turnaround, I asked the agent if there had been a car accident. He laughed and said, "Yeah, right, an accident!" I wasn't sure what he meant, but from his tone, it appeared they needed the ambulances because of trouble at the border.

His dismissive comment came to mind a few days later when I again encountered the Border Patrol. For now, the plan to visit Tombstone was on hold. It would have to wait for another time because I had my appointment the next day to view the apartment.

When I left the hotel the next morning, it was still dark. I approached the ramp to enter the interstate, but it was closed and patrolmen were ushering vehicles to another freeway entrance down the road. An 18-wheel truck carrying six cars had overturned and burned, and the charred wreckage was blocking the ramp; it would take time for the tow trucks to get the road cleared. Later, I wondered if this had been an omen for my day ahead.

Once I got on Interstate 10, I drove in heavy rain to Tucson. My car needed gas, and I wanted a cup of coffee, but it did not appear that many businesses were open. I exited the interstate and found a convenience store that had its lights on. I fueled the car and got a wonderful cup of coffee, which I hadn't expected from a corner market. Getting coffee before the sun comes up must be the secret to getting a fresh brew. The rain stopped somewhere between Tucson and the Tohono O'odham Reservation. The western sky was eerie and dark with clouds as the sun rose behind me.

Curley School Artist Apartments Ajo, AZ

I was excited to get to Ajo and the prospect of a new home in a building with other artists sharing a wood shop, pottery studio, as well as a commercial kitchen. I arrived at the scheduled time and met Vicky, the apartment manager. As we toured the building, my heart sank. I tried to see the benefits of this as my home, but no matter what I told myself, there were too many issues that would not work for me. I knew it was out of the question. So much for *The Plan* that had taken me from my home and familiar surroundings!

By the time we finished the tour of the property, it was late afternoon. The Border Patrol officers had booked all the hotels, but I had done my research and made a reservation at an RV resort. A spot was waiting for me. It was conveniently located by the restrooms, showers, and Wi-Fi connection. It was the smallest site in the park because you don't need a very big space to pitch a tent.

I pulled the tent from the trunk of my Honda Civic and began spreading it out on the ground. Two ladies walking by cheerfully said they used to tent and asked if they could help. These days, I never refuse help! They knew exactly what needed to be done and set to work, while I tried to pound the flimsy metal stakes that came with it into the ground with a rock. The stakes bent and refused to penetrate the rocky soil. I have always camped in the mountains where the soil is soft; I wasn't prepared for this.

I tried moving the stake to the left and right and using different size rocks, to no avail. It was then that my *knight* came to the rescue with a hammer and heavy orange plastic stakes. With a few strokes, he had the tent anchored. He said he used to have a tent similar to mine, and he seemed to enjoy the nostalgia of thinking back to those days. With everyone's help, my new home was quickly set up and anchored securely in the ground.

My helpers returned to their campsites to have dinner, and I started making the inside of the tent cozy. I carried in the blowup mattress, blankets, lamp, computer, and all the other things that make a tent a home. I also had my electric space heater, which puts out warm air, while the plastic casing remains cool. This type of heater is safe to touch and use inside a tent.

When I tried to plug the extension cord into the resort's electric outlet, it didn't fit; I needed an adaptor. How was I going to charge my phone or use the heater? Blowing up the air mattress wasn't a concern, as I had packed the motor that used batteries, as well as the electric one. At least I wouldn't have to sleep on rocks, but anxiety arose at the thought that I may have a chilly night ahead. I hate being cold and suspected that in February the desert temperatures would drop once the sun went down. I asked someone where I could get the part I needed, and it wasn't long before a camper showed up with one I could borrow.

I didn't notice at the time but thinking back on it, my helpers were not housed in big rigs. They were people who had started humbly in a tent and now had modest campers. They knew the challenges that tent life brings, and they were eager to help when they could with exactly what I needed.

The day had taken its toll on me. *The Plan* for my new home was erased from the board of possibilities. My disappointment with the apartment, the effort of getting camp set up, and the stress of seeing the Border Police everywhere had left me exhausted. I love adventure, but this was overwhelming and took me far outside my comfort zone. I wasn't hungry, but I pulled some dinner from the cooler, ate, and went to bed.

The temperature dropped substantially as the sun sank below the mountain. After the sun disappeared, the wind came up and whipped my tent and the rain pounded it. I turned the heater on high. It was wonderful to be curled up in bed with my heater and cuddly blankets, while the tent took the brunt of the elements. I was ever so grateful for the man with the hammer and sturdy orange stakes. I felt safe.

I had survived my first day in the Sonoran Desert, which had left me without a plan! Now what? As I fell asleep, I heard a voice say, "Rest and the answers will come." There was nothing else I could do, so I did!

Little did I know that by now, the campers had tagged me as *The Girl in the Tent*. That name stuck, and they remembered me when I returned months later.

The Takeaway: Sometimes we have to let The Plan go.

Story 2
My Safe Space

Many children pull the cushions off the sofa, gather blankets and pillows, and create a fort on the living room floor. What compels them to do this? What do they do in their tent once they get it built? Is it fun playing in it, or do they immediately tear it down and make another? No matter what they do, it certainly keeps them entertained, but is there more to it? I suspect it's different for all children, but I wonder if others are like I was. My real story wasn't that I built tents, but why I built them and what happened when I was inside.

My tenting began when I was five years old after my mother died. Her passing contributed to me never feeling safe or at ease. After her transition, there was a parade of people in and out of our house whose job was to care for my three siblings and me in exchange for food and lodging. Most of them wanted a free place to stay and did not care about us kids.

Things were chaotic and being a sensitive child, I did the only thing I could to escape; I built a tent and retreated into it when things became overwhelming.

Our house was small, and I was not allowed to build one in the living room, so my first tent was in my bed. I built towers with my TinkerToys and put them in bed with me to raise the blankets, making my little space. I instinctively knew that I needed a place to have time out from the world, and in my mind, no one could see me here, so they would leave me alone. And they did.

Later, when my dad built an addition to the house, he had large insulation boxes and he allowed me to have one. One end was the door, and I made a window on the opposite end by tearing the cardboard. After I climbed into the box with my doll Susie and her blankets, I closed the door flaps. My box became a special place for us in the yard away from the chaos, and since I was small, it felt quite roomy.

I'd lie in there for long periods, staring out the makeshift window at the sky, watching the clouds float and form into different shapes. Sometimes there were puffy clouds, and behind them, smooth clouds. Some looked like my breath when I exhaled on winter days. Others looked like huge cotton balls, angels, faces, or dogs. I would fall into a peaceful sleep while playing in heaven's creations.

When the rain ruined my box and it smelled bad, I went to the vacant lot next door. In the field, the weeds were shoulder-high, and when I lay down, no one could see me. They would not look for me as long as I was back in the house when my dad got home. They didn't care where I was; at least I wasn't underfoot.

As I lay there, the cricket's song, the grasshopper's clicking sounds, and the ladybugs crawling up the plants soothed me. I gazed at clouds as they floated across the sky, and soon I drifted into daydreams that took me far beyond the confines of my little body.

After my sister discovered my hiding place in the field, Nana's yard became my refuge. Her house was on the block next to ours, so our yards backed up to each other. I often spent time with her eating freshly baked goodies and drinking hand-squeezed lemonade. We did not have these treasured treats at our house. Nana and I played jacks, Chinese checkers, and Parcheesi. I usually won, possibly because she let me, although I was pretty proud of my abilities.

My Beloved Nana

She knew my love of tents and built a wooden A-frame with blue and red blankets for the sides. It is probably politically incorrect today, but back then, they were called Indian blankets, though I am not sure why. She assembled it on her lush green lawn. It was in front of her home, out of view of the masses that gathered at my house. She allowed me to take her blankets outside to the tent so Susie, my baby doll, and I were quite comfortable.

I Love my Baby Doll

Susie was my best friend and went everywhere with me. She had a ceramic head with eyes that opened and closed. She had short, brown, curly hair. Her legs and arms were ceramic and her body was cloth. Her face and legs had chips in them, but I didn't care; I bandaged them and told her she would be okay. I could feel a hard object in her chest that said "Mama" when I picked her up.

Susie and I spent hours in the space that Nana had created for us. Often, Nana brought ham sandwiches and her wonderful homemade chocolate chip cookies out, so Susie and I could have a tea party. Sometimes she crawled into the tent and joined us.

Nana's yard was a magical, quiet place where all I heard were birds singing, squirrels chattering and an occasional car driving by on the gravel road. I loved this space, which differed greatly from my house. My grandma was a blessing in my life. She knew and understood what I needed, and she provided a calm, safe environment for me.

I never minded being alone, as it was usually preferable to the alternative. My tenting experiences saved me as a child. I napped but never spent the night outside in a tent until I was a teenager, which I will tell you about in another Story.

Tents shaped my love of nature and showed me the importance of having a place where I could go to get away from the chaos of life and recharge. Even today, when I am camping, I feel renewed and at peace. At five years old, I could not have articulated this, but I knew the feeling well.

The Takeaway: At any age, it is well to have a safe space to revitalize the body and mind.

Story 3
Organ Pipe Cactus Monument

Since the apartment at Curley School didn't work out and I no longer had a home to return to, I didn't know what my next step was. There was nowhere I needed to be, and I was enjoying the people at the RV park, so I stayed for a while to be a tourist.

Saguaro Cactus in Organ Pipe Cactus National Monument

The Organ Pipe Cactus National Monument was only twenty miles away and would make a nice trip, so I made that my destination for the day. The United Nations designated this area as the International Biosphere Reserve in 1976 and made it part of the national park system. It is a nature preserve, so they protect it to allow its unique ecosystem to survive unspoiled.

The magnificent saguaro cactus that are so prominent grow extremely slow. The tallest recorded reached 78 feet, but most never grow over 45 feet, taking about 200 years. Some have many arms and some only have a few. They survive in the heat because they have a five-foot taproot and many smaller roots closer to the surface that all gather water. Their waxy skin helps them retain moisture in the scorching desert sun.

Plants of the Sonoran Desert

Besides the saguaro, thirty other species of cactus grow in this area. There is also a thriving community of other plants and animals that have adapted to living in this harsh environment, many of which only reveal themselves after dark.

To get to the visitor's center, I would have to go through the border checkpoint, which is on U.S. soil and serves as the entry and exit point between the U.S. and Mexico. This would be my first crossing since the construction of the border wall in this area began, and I was anxious about going there. I inched my way up the line of vehicles and saw at least six cameras pointed at my car. That seemed excessive.

Dogs were on patrol and signs warned not to approach them. No worries, I would not get out of my car unless ordered to. I kept my hands on the wheel and tried not to look anxious, despite my unnerving encounter with the Border Patrol on the road to Tombstone a few days earlier. I thought fear would imply guilt, and I did not want to attract that kind of attention, so I told myself to stay cool.

I watched as vehicles coming from Mexico were directed to the side of the road, people were told to get out, and then they and their cars were searched. Witnessing this did not instill confidence in me or add comfort to the thought of what would happen when I reached the guards. I was tempted to forget the trip to the visitors' center and turn around, but I thought that would surely attract unwanted attention, so I continued slowly moving forward.

Sign by Arizona/Mexico Border

When I reached the patrolmen, one asked if I was a U.S. citizen. I said, "Yes," and he waved me through. I thought, "And you were all worried about nothing!" It was then that I realized the cameras had taken my picture, and the computer had run my license plate number before I ever got to the guards. They knew I was a great-grandma from South Dakota who had car insurance, was of average height and weight, wasn't on a terrorist list, and posed no threat. Did this make me leery of or grateful for technology? I wasn't sure.

I drove to the visitors' center, walked around the exhibits, and listened to a ranger talk about snakes and plants. There didn't seem to be anywhere to purchase a meal, so the lunch I had packed was most welcome. After snapping lots of photos, I prepared to drive back across the border, wondering what my experience would be as I drove from Mexico's side into the U.S.

It took much longer to drive back through the checkpoint because of the number of vehicles that were being searched. My car was loaded with gear, and I dreaded the thought that I'd have to empty it for them, but I tried not to think about that. After all, I had technology on my side.

Following a long wait in line, I arrived at the guards and they waved me through. Was it my grandmotherly face or did technology again do its job? The visitors' center was interesting, but I can't say it was the highlight of my day. Getting there and back was what made a huge impression on me.

As I drove back to Ajo, the sun was setting, and the sky started its light show. It was magnificent! The golds, pinks, and oranges spread across the horizon, turning the saguaros into mere shadows. After taking more photos, I returned to my tent tired, relieved, and feverish. This fever was to become familiar to me during my time in Ajo.

The Takeaway: Like it or not, technology surrounds us, and sometimes it can be useful.

Story 4
Biosphere II

Mabel lived north of Phoenix, and we had not seen each other since we both lived in Colorado years before. It was time to reconnect, so she would drive to Ajo, spend the night, and we would go to Biosphere II in Oracle, Arizona, the next day.

It was a welcome reunion. We consumed the dinner I had prepared, and when the sun was getting low, we discussed sleeping arrangements. Mabel had decided not to bring her camping gear, and I did not have extra, so the only thing to do was for her to sleep in her car.

The back seat folded down, and it seemed a good idea to stretch out with her legs in the trunk. That lasted about five minutes until she slid into the trunk. That was not going to work. Sleeping in the driver's seat seemed like the best option, and that is where she spent the night.

In the night, I awoke to the sound of the engine starting as she warmed the car. I doubted she was having a good sleep. I was quite cozy in my tent and felt guilty, but I also didn't know what I could do. I had spent nights in my car in cold weather and knew it was not comfortable.

When I got up in the morning, I checked on her and she was curled up behind the steering wheel hidden by blankets; I was sure it had been a short night for her. I made coffee and tapped on her window. After a breakfast of eggs and French toast, we left for the Biosphere. We each drove our car, as we would go in opposite directions when we left the Biosphere.

I had heard of the Biosphere when it first opened in 1991, and it had been my long-held desire to go there. A mini-Earth with a rainforest, savannah, agricultural garden, marsh, and ocean reef biomes seemed like science fiction, and I was finally getting to experience it firsthand!

Biosphere I, Earth

Biosphere I is Earth itself. Biosphere II is a three-acre, sealed glass-and-steel ecological research center built between 1987 and 1991 to learn about Earth, its biomes, and how they interact when temperature, humidity, and air are all controlled. Perhaps its greatest purpose was to learn what some challenges would be living in an off-planet colony. To gather this information, they built the Biosphere to resemble and operate like a giant terrarium.

In 1991, eight people, each with their area of expertise, said goodbye to their families and sealed themselves inside the air-tight structure where they would live for two years. Their only communication with the outside world was by email, phone, and fax as there was no Zoom, Facetime, or even Skype at that time. They brought everything they needed with them or grew it inside the facility. Air, water, and waste were all recycled, making this a self-contained environment.

Biosphere II, Oracle, AZ

The Biosphere was not without its issues. Partway into their stay, oxygen levels fell, and it had to be pumped in from outside to protect the inhabitants. Many of the garden plants died, so for the first six months, the crew was always hungry. They lost weight, but that later stabilized and they regained some of it, as they adjusted to the low-calorie, nutrient-dense diet.

When the doctors examined them after leaving the Biosphere, their overall well-being proved that this type of diet can increase health and longevity. However, it did little to support their emotional health. This crew left after two years.

In 1994, another group attempted to live in the Biosphere, but two of the members sabotaged the system and it forced the people to leave after six months.

While these missions did not accomplish all the scientists had hoped, many important data came from the experiments that helped in the studies of ecology, atmospheric science, soils, and climate change. They still use the facility for research and education, and I was excited that I was going to be educated!

As we waited for our tour group to be called, I examined the displays in the lobby. There was a room off the main one with a display of hand-cast paper items that children had made. Years before this, I was a papermaker, so their creativity interested me.

When our group was called, we followed the guide. He led us past the aquaponics display, through the biomes, and down to the technosphere below. There we saw enormous pieces of equipment, water pipes, electrical lines, pumps, and motors that were all needed to do what the Earth does every day.

Biosphere II from the Inside Looking Out

29

All I saw fascinated me, but two things stood out. One was a tall tree that could not stand erect because it had grown too quickly and was softer wood than its outdoor counterparts. It had not experienced the elements of nature like the wind to make it grow strong. It had to be tied to the beams to keep it from toppling over. The scientists had replicated nature inside the Biosphere, but they hadn't accounted for the role elements like wind play. The metaphor of how challenges in our lives make us strong did not escape me.

The other outstanding item was that the structure breathed! Since the desert heats during the day and cools at night, the pressure inside the facility could change substantially, thereby putting much stress on the glass. To solve this, the engineers designed a *lung* to regulate the pressure.

The Lung

The lung looked like a giant spaceship. It was a huge metal plate with legs. The plate was connected to a rubber membrane that moved up and down with the air pressure. It moved slowly, but it did appear to be breathing. As we entered the area that housed the lung, we were sucked into the room. While in the room, it felt quite normal, but when we left by another door, we were ejected out of the building. Of course, no one was injured, but it was a surprise and it seemed a novel way to end a tour.

They made many discoveries through the experiments conducted in the Biosphere. From the coral reef, scientists learned much about the impact of increased CO_2 and ocean acidification on global climate change. Another contribution was the work done with recycling the crew and animal waste through low-tech filtration methods. This led to the development of an inexpensive water treatment system that is now used in developing countries. Although they learned much, life in the Biosphere made it obvious there was still a lot we don't know about human relations and this planet we call home.

After the tour, Mabel and I went to the main building for a snack in the cafeteria and to unwrap what we had just experienced. We didn't stay long as the sun was getting low and it was time to part company. We commented on how wise we had been to drive separately since she would go north to her home and me south to Ajo. It had been a long day, and after her night in the car, I was sure she was happily imagining a good night's sleep in her bed.

It had been a day filled with many wonderful experiences. As I drove up to my 10′ x 10′ tent, I exhaled a long sigh. I was grateful to get back to my little desert home. I had a snack and went into my tent.

My Desert Home

As I lay in my bed, I gave thanks for the wonders this life offers. The sounds of nearby coyotes and hooting owls soothed me. I slept.

The Takeaway: Our planet contains many wonders we have yet to discover.

Story 5
Canyonlands Vision Quest

There was no plan, and I accepted that, although it was not easy. From experience, I knew I *would* know, and that I just needed to be patient until the time was right. I learned that from a previous camping experience in the Canyonlands of Utah.

At that time, I was living in Boulder, Colorado, and I was feeling restless; I needed direction. How could I use the energy of discontent to change my life? My answer was to take a break and get away; time in nature always helped.

I thought about where to go, and it was still too cold to go to the mountains, so I looked to the desert. The desert is inspirational with its colors, rock formations, dryness, expansive blue sky, and magnificent sunsets. As I thought about it, I felt at peace, so the desert it was. But which desert?

I remembered the wonderful time our family had when we took a boat trip on the Green River in Utah. After consulting the road atlas, the Canyonlands just south of Moab *lit up*, and I knew that was where I needed to go. With camping gear loaded in Rocky, my 1990 black Geo Prizm, I headed west to find the perfect place to unwind and get clarity. Rocky and I had traveled over 200,000 miles together, and she was always ready for another road trip.

I drove west on Interstate 70 through the Rocky Mountains to Highway 128, where I turned toward Moab. As I drove beside the Colorado River, I considered a spot there, but there were many anglers camped in those sites and it was right next to the highway. I knew the noise of the campers and traffic would distract me, so I kept driving and continued with my plan to go to the Canyonlands. I turned south onto Highway 191.

I drove into the Canyonlands National Park. The Green and Colorado Rivers encircle the park and its sandstone spires create stunning desert vistas. There are campgrounds in the park, but that was not the environment I was looking for. I kept driving. I needed to find the right spot. It had to be away from traffic and people. I explored the area, not sure what I was looking for, but trusted I would know it when I saw it.

Canyonlands Vista

One of the gravel roads I followed was alongside flowing water and canopied by immense cottonwood trees. It could have been a creek or a small river, but whatever it was, it looked inviting. There was only one person nearby, and the space seemed to meet my campsite criteria. I made camp.

The steep canyon walls on either side were beautiful, but two things I had not considered; in a canyon, you have a limited view of the sky, and the sun disappears early and comes up late, making for long, chilly nights at that time of year.

I was missing out on the wonders of the desert, so one night in this spot was enough; it was time to move to a sunny location where I could see the sunset and the night sky. I dismantled my camp and repacked the car. Further down the road, not knowing exactly where I was other than the backcountry, a sign informed me this was Bureau of Land Management (BLM) Public Land. BLM is open land where you can throw a sleeping bag on the ground anywhere you want and sleep under the stars.

I turned onto another road, which was more red dirt than gravel, and drove deeper into BLM territory. On my right, there was a small rock formation that looked ideal. It provided raised areas I could use for my table and seating. This was it! It looked perfect, but was it?

This stay in the desert was an ideal time to do what my Native American friend called a *vision quest*. Vision quests are usually undertaken by young boys as their rite of passage, but it seemed to me it would be a good thing for anyone to do at any age. It primarily consists of fasting and spending three days alone in a quiet place, to still the mind and open to a vision. Some protocols, like fasting, did not fit my circumstances, so I created my version of the ritual.

I stepped out of the car and surveyed the area to determine what space I would claim as mine for the next three days. Once I determined where that would be, I drew a large circle with a stick. It was big enough to accommodate the rock formation, plus a bit beyond to keep me from feeling confined. I intended that nothing and no one would enter this circle, and I would not go outside of it while I was involved in my quest. After I finished the circle, I set up camp.

There was no shade in the area other than under the desert sage plants, which were way too short to provide cover for anything bigger than a lizard. I didn't want to be in full sun all day because of the risk of sunburn. I looked at my tent and realized, that by pulling back the flaps in a certain way, I could see out and the breeze could flow through, sheltering me from the intense midday sun. This is where I spent my afternoons.

Once I put everything in order, I set my intention for my vision quest. I never do things small and I decided to explore my birth story and heal my birth trauma. To help me with this, I would use the book, *Bonds of Fire,* by Dr. Alice Rose. It is about birth and in-utero trauma. It discussed what can happen to us before birth and how that can affect our lives. I had heard Dr. Rose speak in Denver and the premise interested me. This would be an uninterrupted opportunity to delve into the information and my story.

Bonds of Fire by Dr. Alice Rose

One statement in the book read, "Without question and without exception, birth is the single most
traumatic moment in our lives." I have had many traumatic events in my life, and this statement strongly res-
onated with me. As I read, I allowed tears, fears, grief,
and pain to come up; I stopped nothing from rising to
the surface. The energy of the quest and my desire to
clear my birth trauma were strong and guided me
through the process.

It is hard to explain all that happened inside of
me, other than to say I experienced being in the womb
and I was aware of my birth. I could fast-forward
through my life and see how these things influenced me
and my experiences. My days and nights were filled
with realizations, thoughts, and dreams that helped me
clear this part of my past.

I walked around the space I had marked off. I
prepared simple meals and slept a lot. I watched the
sunsets as they quietly highlighted the rocky desert
formations with a palette of colors that swept across the

sky. I say *quietly* only because, if you weren't looking, you would miss the sky in its glory.

The night heavens reflected my inner work. Without the city lights, the blackness and the millions of stars were otherworldly. The Big Dipper filled the northern sky and formed a giant question mark standing on its handle. Rather naively, I was sure the stars positioned themselves like that just for me.

The spirits of the vision quest were protecting me. When I entered my tent at night, a big yellow spirit dog came to keep watch outside my door. The Natives would probably call him my spirit animal. He left in the morning. I was never afraid. It all felt very mystical and yet very real.

Early one morning, as I lay awake in bed, I heard sounds in my protected area. It sounded like my camp was being ransacked. I wasn't about to leave the tent and anger whatever was out there. When the noise stopped, and I emerged from the safety of my tent, I saw that something had tossed my camp. A few things were missing, but the only thing of importance was my toothbrush. I didn't know what kind of critter needed a toothbrush or was big enough to carry it off, but I had to get another. This meant I would have to leave my sacred circle.

The day before, I had passed a convenience store down the road, so I went there. I told the shopkeeper my story, and she chuckled as she informed me it was a packrat that took it; they are common in the area and take many strange things from campers. She didn't have any brushes on the shelves, but she went to her apartment in the back of the store and brought out a spare she had. It was still wrapped in plastic. I offered to pay her, but she laughed and said, "No charge." I went back to camp and put my treasure in the car, so we didn't have a repeat performance. The packrats did not return.

A Packrat

I had set up my circle of protection and wondered how they were able to enter it. I contemplated it for a minute and then realized they hadn't entered it; they lived in it! The rock formation was their home, and I had drawn my circle around it and included them in it.

Time passed quickly without my being aware that it had. I had no human contact for three days, except for the lady at the store and a wave of greeting I exchanged with people in the car that passed by.

At the end of the three days, I was ready to leave. I had achieved my objective, and it was time to pack my things and leave the circle. I closed the circle, expressing appreciation to the space and all of nature for the support that had allowed me to do my inner work. I felt renewed and ready for my next adventure. I didn't know exactly what that was, but I did know I needed to contact a friend who lived in Santa Fe.

When I reached a payphone (cell phones had not become popular), I called my friend, and she said she had been trying to reach me, as her mother-in-law was ill and preparing to pass over. Since I had been a hospice volunteer, she thought I would be a great help in taking care of her.

I had my answer and knew what to do next; I drove to Santa Fe. Three weeks later, her mother-in-law gently slipped out of her body.

As a result of being there, opportunities opened up that caused significant changes in my life that I never could have anticipated. But that is another story.

I found it interesting that I had spent my three-day vision quest exploring the birth process and the next three weeks looking at death. Somehow, it seemed appropriate.

The Takeaway: If life is overwhelming, get quiet, and look at the sky. And keep your things picked up so the critters don't steal them.

Story 6
No Plan Is The Plan

My life felt surreal. I was present in each moment, perhaps more than ever before, but it seemed I was swimming from one unrelated event to another. I didn't know what was coming from moment to moment, so whatever came, there I was. It was less than a month since I had left my home in South Dakota, yet it could have been a year, perhaps more. I had lost track of time, and the concept of it meant nothing to me.

Before I went to sleep at night, I asked if I was to leave my location the next day, and if so, what direction should I point my car. No answers were forthcoming. It probably didn't make any difference if I had a plan, as the ones I did have weren't working out anyway.

I enjoyed making plans. It was fun to walk through different scenarios in my mind, see the possibilities, and research each phase. I liked the process, and I confess I was more comfortable having a plan, even if it was just a short-term one. My feeling has always been to have a strategy and remain flexible with change when it comes. That I could easily do, but having *no* plan or destination was another story. Mark Twain expressed my state well.

> *Why do you sit there looking like an*
> *envelope without any address on it?*
> Mark Twain

41

This wasn't just about making modifications; there was no plan at all. Not knowing till the last minute what to do or where to go was difficult to accept, but as I got more practice, it did get easier.

It was interesting to see how worked up I could get trying to find a decision that the mind was not equipped to make; it just didn't have all the facts or the experience on which to base a proper choice. As I saw what came when I had no expectations was always better than I could have imagined, it helped. Seeing this play out over and over helped me build confidence that the new way worked and was a good thing.

While I grappled with this, life did its part to uplift me so I could stay the course. A song, a person, or an animal was there to say or do exactly what I needed. When these things happened, it may have seemed coincidental to an observer, but to me, there was nothing coincidental about it.

One such instance was when I needed a boost and turned on the radio, the song *When You're Going Through Hell,* by Rodney Atkins, was playing, or it was the next song that came up. Several times, it was even playing over the loudspeaker at gas stations while I pumped gas. I loved this song and sang it with a volume that was probably unbecoming of a lady. I felt it in my core. The chorus lyrics are:

> *If you're going through hell, keep on going,*
> *Don't slow down, if you're scared don't show it.*
> *You might get out before the devil even knows*
> *you're there.*

If you're going through hell, keep on moving,
Face that fire, walk right through it.
You might get out before the devil even knows
you're there.

It felt good to be reassured that if I just kept going, I would get through whatever challenge was up that day. This song, along with the mantra, "Rest and the answers will come," pulled me through some doubtful times.

Other things happened like the morning I sat at my campsite drinking coffee and contemplating if it was time to leave and it started raining. That was my answer, as there was no way I wanted to pack up the wet gear. I would spend the day in my tent and just be still. I could use the quiet time because no matter how much sleep I had, I still woke up feeling bone tired, a weariness I could not identify, but I knew it came from deep inside.

The fever I had been experiencing off and on was also back. I wasn't sure if it was from being in the desert sun, or if I was ill. I felt exhausted, had a hard time keeping warm, and my body hurt, but I did not feel sick. Whatever the cause, it seemed important to take time to rest. I did not have a plan, so this must be the day's course of action. The words of Winnie the Pooh came to mind.

Sometimes, the thing to do is nothing.
The Wisdom of Pooh Bear

In my quiet time, I asked what I had gained from my experience in the desert. The first realization was that I had suspected the desert could get chilly in February, but I had not imagined the warm days could turn to extreme wind and rain once the sun disappeared. Of course, it was not like South Dakota, but you expect it there and don't spend a February night in a tent! I did smile though because I had the foresight to pack my tent heater and waterproof my tent. At least, it stayed toasty warm inside even when the wind blew so hard the fabric flapped and the structure bent almost to the ground.

The second thing I learned is if you want to be part of a community, get out of your comfort zone and talk to people, take a class, join a church, or volunteer. There were discussion groups, dance, weaving, pottery, gardening, and book clubs to investigate. Most of the people who stayed in the area for a few months took part in these events. On this trip, I was content to spend my time experiencing the town and culture at my pace. However, when I later returned, I did volunteer for the International Sonoran Desert Alliance (ISDA).

My third realization was that if I was going to do more RV park tenting, I needed to get the foam squares I had seen in the children's play area at the library to pad the floor of my tent, as my knees were red and sore from crawling in and out. When I camped in the mountains, the ground was soft with leaves and pine needles, but here it was hard gravel. I also needed heavier tent stakes, a hammer, and an electrical adaptor.

I can't say these were great revelations, but it was good information. I was tired and achy, but couldn't sleep, so when the rain stopped, I went for a walk on the outskirts of town to work the stiffness out of my body. I took my camera, but the lighting was dull and there wasn't much I wanted to photograph, so I went back to my tent and lay down. I told myself I would go back out at sunset for photos and I drifted off to sleep.

As I slid into blessed slumber, the movie *Eat, Pray, Love* came to mind and I knew what it meant to experience the *sweetness of doing nothing*. I slept deeply and woke as the sun's golden hues filled my tent; I knew it was fading over the hill. I had the delicious feeling of total comfort and completeness. I rolled over and went back to sleep. No photos tonight. Blessed sleep!

Sometimes when I'm going somewhere and I wait,
a somewhere comes to me.
The Wisdom of Pooh Bear

I slept through the night and I awoke in the morning knowing I was going to Phoenix to visit family. After a phone call, I knew when I should arrive. It was time to pack up my tent and leave this area. I had a destination!

The Takeaway: Be patient and let the plan reveal itself.

Story 7
Tombstone and Bisbee

Tombstone was still on my mind. Since I couldn't visit there on my way to Ajo, I decided to go before I went to Phoenix and left southern Arizona. Tombstone was out of the way, but if I was to get there, this was the logical time to go.

The shortest route to Tombstone from Ajo was to drive across the Tohono O'Odham reservation. The reservation had become a major crossing area for people illegally entering the U.S. from Mexico, and the activity was highest between dusk and dawn. I was told it was best to travel during daylight hours to avoid potential issues. I kept this in mind as I timed my trip.

Sign near the Mexican Border in Arizona

The 150 miles to Tombstone through the reservation took more than the two and a half hours my GPS projected because I stopped many times. There were few structures, but the saguaro cactus fascinated me. Their arms mostly reached to the sky, but some seemed to go every which direction.

Saguaro Cactus

There were also roadside memorials, or *descansos* as they are known in Spanish, that demanded my attention.

Descanso

Descanso means *resting place* and descansos are shrines that mark the passing of a loved one. There is usually a cross planted in the soil, and there might be a bicycle, pictures of the deceased, statues of Jesus or Mary, military awards, plaques, flags, flowers, or anything that reminds the family of their loved one and pays tribute to them. Between the cactus and shrines, I stopped many times to take photos.

In the next picture, I did not notice the white van in the upper right corner until I was posting it here. It probably was a Border Patrol van.

Descansos in Arizona

The Border Patrol appeared often in the brush. I wondered why they were riding their ATVs in the weeds, but decided it must be to flush out anyone hiding there. By now, I was getting more at ease seeing them everywhere and knew they had all the information they needed about me through profiling and technology.

However, I wondered if they would stop me to see what I was doing. They didn't. I reasoned they

48

didn't want to waste their time when they had more important things to investigate.

Tombstone had always interested me. I grew up with western movies and many were set in Tombstone, Arizona, so I had often seen it portrayed in black and white on the big screen and thought it would be fun to go there.

Tombstone, founded in 1877, was known as the *Town too Tough to Die*, which was proven when fires nearly destroyed it twice and the silver mine flooded and had to close. People lost their income and many moved away. Despite that, the town survived. In 1957, the movie *Shootout at OK Corral* breathed new life into this legendary town.

The 1881 gunfight, which we know as taking place at the OK Corral, did not take place there but in a vacant lot on Fremont Street. One interesting thing about the gunfight is that it was over in 24 seconds.

Tombstone had its historical figures like Doc Holliday and Wyatt Earp, who fought in this famous gunfight along with Wyatt's brothers, Morgan and Virgil. The four survived the fight, but Morgan and Virgil were later shot in retaliation. Morgan was killed and Virgil was maimed. Wyatt and Doc Holliday left town soon after that.

After traveling around the west, Wyatt settled in Los Angeles where he died, and Holliday went to Glenwood Springs, Colorado, to recuperate from tuberculosis, and that is where he died at age 36. After reading headstones and accounts of the Old West, it appears people didn't live long in those days.

The history of Tombstone reminded me of Deadwood, South Dakota, which was founded in 1876, one year before Tombstone. It was known for its role in the Black Hills gold rush, and because of that, became a National Historic Landmark in 1961. Over the years, it burned three times and flooded once. These events, plus the economic problems it was facing, left it on the verge of becoming a ghost town. It was spared this fate in 1989 when gambling was legalized, making it the third legal gaming destination in the United States, after Nevada and Atlantic City.

They keep the memory of the Wild West alive in Deadwood each summer when actors perform gunfights on the main street. Tourists line the sidewalks to watch and then they visit Mount Moriah Cemetery to see the burial sites of Seth Bullock, Wild Bill, Calamity Jane, Potato Creek Johnny, and other notable figures.

Wild Bill's Headstone

Calamity Jane's Headstone

Presently, Wild Bill Hickok and Calamity Jane are buried next to each other, but that was not always so.

Wild Bill's body was moved, but the reason is unclear. Some say his body was relocated so the land he was on could be developed. And some say it was to keep the legend alive that he and Calamity Jane were lovers, but supposedly, they didn't even like each other. And some say it was Calamity Jane's last wish to be buried next to Wild Bill, and since she died after him, her wish was honored. We are left to draw our own conclusions.

Visitors can enjoy a beer and dance in the No. 10 Saloon where Wild Bill was shot in the back by Jack McCall, *Broken Nose Jack* in 1876. The old hotels are open for bookings, should one want that experience. You get a real feeling of life in the Old West when you are there, and the charge for the experience is little or nothing.

Having experienced that authentic Old West town, I had high expectations of Tombstone, but as similar as their histories were, they preserve that history differently.

Boothill Graveyard, Tombstone, AZ

Tombstone keeps its history alive with staged gunfights that are scheduled around town. There is also

Boothill Graveyard, where outlaws were buried, but no well-known figures were laid to rest there.

According to the guide, the Bird Cage Theatre, which was a brothel and gambling hall, is the only original building left downtown, and you can see the interior if you take the tour. There are interesting things to see around Tombstone, like the original courthouse, museums, old churches, and the Good Enough Mine. They have commercialized most of the attractions and you can experience them for a price.

Bird Cage Theatre

While the town was not as intact and authentic as I had hoped, the land surrounding Tombstone impressed me. It was exactly as I had imagined! Cactus and sagebrush cover the hills, which may not sound exciting, but it brought back memories of the westerns I had seen so long ago. I could easily imagine the cowboys and gunslingers riding across the desert and arriving in town hot, thirsty for whiskey, and ready for action.

I saw many western movies as a kid. On wintery Sunday afternoons, Dad dropped my sister and me off at the movie theater. It didn't matter what was showing, but it was usually a western. One thing for sure was that it was in black and white; technicolor didn't come until later. Dad gave us each a dime, five cents to get in and five cents for popcorn. He dropped us off after dinner (what people today call lunch) and picked us up two hours later. Often, we got there in time to see the end of the movie and then we would stay and watch the beginning. But we didn't care; it was a treat to go to the movie, plus we didn't know any other way.

When I felt complete with my tour of Tombstone, I continued south 25 miles to Bisbee, which is a small art community. A sign greeted me claiming, "Bisbee has the best year-round climate on Earth." Its southern location and high altitude combine to make desirable weather a reality.

It is a picturesque town that reminded me of Manitou Springs, Colorado. They both began as mining towns and are now art communities with little boutique shops. They were both built on the side of a mountain in the late 1800s. The streets are steep and there are many steps to the homes staggered up the hillside.

Mural in Bisbee, AZ

My tour of Bisbee began at the visitors' center. I learned Bisbee is a former copper mining town. The mine closed in 1975 after 100 years of operation.

Fly Swatting Contest Article

In the early 1900s, there was a fly-swatting competition held each year to control the number of flies that carried typhoid. The flies could be captured by any means, but they had to be placed in a cardboard box for the judges. In 1912, the winner bagged 5,000 of the 50,000 flies that were caught. I wondered how many people volunteered to count these disease-infested insects to judge the contest!

As I walked around town, I noticed the buildings were brick, not the wood that most of the old towns used. This wasn't always the case, but after the fourth major fire in 1908, they rebuilt with brick to keep the town from burning down again. There were no fatalities in the 1908 fire, but the next day, a man was passing an adobe wall that was still standing and a gust of wind blew it over, crushing him. This town seemed to have some strange stories to tell!

I huffed and puffed as I walked up the hill. I couldn't help but think I would be in really great shape if I lived there, but if the truth be told, I would probably let my car get the workout.

Many of the eclectic art galleries and shops that I passed were closed, but I went into those that were open to examine the unique items they had displayed. There were oil and acrylic paintings, pottery, decorative wall tiles, paintings that appeared to have jewels embedded in them, and dishes that were filled with epoxy and looked like a blue or orange beta was swimming in them. They looked so lifelike that my first thought was, "That poor fish is confined to a tiny space." The artists used tried-and-true media in unique ways to create one-of-a-kind items.

Resin Beta in Bowl

The most fascinating person I met was David Kachel, a photographer who calls himself an art photographer because of the many artistic things he does with his photographs. He works with black and white photos, direct-to-plate, polymer photogravure, and dry film polymer photogravure, to name a few. These processes were foreign to me, but I loved the finished products.

I visited with other proprietors who were happy to talk about their merchandise and what it was like to live in this small community. It seems there are mixed feelings about residing in Bisbee.

Some people loved living there and others felt they had come there and got stuck. Some made a good living, and some had trouble eking out a bare existence. What I took from my conversations was that it just depended on each person and the good fortune they had; there was no simple answer.

This was one place I had considered moving to, but after being there, I decided it was a fun place to visit, but it would not work for me to live in that town.

Daylight was waning, and it was time to leave. I drove back through Tombstone and north to Benson, where I got a room for the night. I would continue to Phoenix the next day.

The Takeaway: Townspeople of the Southwest have found creative ways to survive, and learning how they do this can be fun and educational.

Story 8
Lawson's Landing

After visiting with family in Phoenix, I drove west to San Diego, California, and continued up the coast. I took my time and stopped many times to visit areas I had not been to in many years, like San Diego Safari Park, Santa Barbara, and Morro Bay, and then on to Ano Nuevo State Park.

The Pacific Ocean was as gray as the sky when I drove onto the Pacific Coast Highway. My wipers rubbed as they moved intermittently across the windshield, clearing the mist with each swipe.

Pacific Ocean

Many years before this trip, I lived and worked in the San Francisco Bay Area and had been to Ano Nuevo with Don, a coworker, to see the elephant seals. That was also a winter day but, unlike today, the sun was warm and shining brightly. Don and I checked in at the visitors' center desk and were glad we had reservations, as many people were waiting for a tour. The ranger called our group. He told us the protocols for walking among the seals and talked about them as we walked to the beach.

Elephant seals earned that name because of their massive size, their trunk-like proboscis, and their resemblance to elephants when they are swimming. They weigh up to four tons. Their bodies are covered with blubber, which helps them stay warm in the cold, ocean water. They spend about 80% of their time in the ocean, coming ashore in the winter to give birth and mate and then again in the spring to molt. On land, they do not move around much, but they can travel up to five miles per hour if threatened.

It surprised me there were no fences. Seeing these massive bodies rolling around in the sand making growling sounds was frightening, but I trusted the guide knew what he was doing as he led us through the sea of bodies.

Don and I were there during the season when the adult seals were on shore to give birth and breed. I hoped to see these magnificent creatures up close again on this trip, but I was disappointed to find they had finished their yearly ritual and had swum back out to sea; only the pups remained. They would be there until April. By that time, they would have gained weight and grown a new coat of fur that would insulate them from the cold water of the Pacific Ocean. Once they were ready, they would make their way into the sea.

On this day, it was cold and the drizzle was turning to rain, so I opted not to take the three-mile walk out to where the babies lined the beach. Instead, I examined the visitors' center, which offered many displays and informational videos. After an hour of exploration in the center, I drove further up the coast to an ocean overlook.

As I parked, I noticed people were leaning over the railing, looking at something and pointing. Of course, I had to see what the attraction was. I walked to where they were standing and discovered they were watching baby elephant seals. To call them *babies* is misleading, as these pups were now a few months old and no longer had their 75-pound, black, furry bodies. They looked more like the adult harbor seals I had seen at Sea World.

Young Elephant Seals Scuffling

Some were resting on the beach and several males were challenging each other, all the while making low guttural vocalizations. There were hundreds of them at this beach. It turned out I didn't have to take the long, wet walk at the State Park to see them; they were right there! I could view them and take photos without getting wet.

The Pacific Coast Highway has always been a favorite drive, as it is one of the most scenic roads in the world. The cypress trees, rugged coastline, beaches, seagulls, and endless sky are meant to be savored and enjoyed, and the two-lane road ensures that you do.

There are many things to see and smells you don't experience anywhere else, like moist, unpolluted sea air. The freshness of the air makes one want to breathe it in. Driving the coast would not be complete without stopping at a diner to enjoy farm-fresh food, the day's seafood catch, and a wonderful glass of local wine.

Not totally forgetting my quest for a new home in a warmer climate, I asked myself as I drove through the coastal towns if I would like to live there. Being rejuvenated by walking on the beach and breathing the moist sea air is wonderful, but I determined that, while I love visiting this area, it was not to be my home.

When I reached Pescadero, I wasn't far from the redwood forests and there was no question that I would stop for a hike. When I lived in the Bay Area, I hiked Sam McDonald Park hundreds of times. It had always been calming, yet invigorating, to trek through the magical redwoods where it felt like any moment Bilbo Baggins would pop out of a hollow stump.

Some of these giant trees have black scorch marks on their bark from fires that have passed through over the years and moss now clings to the weakened trees. There is a smell in this forest that is unlike others; even similar woods do not smell the same. There is, however, an earthiness that is common to all redwood forests.

A Path through the Redwoods
Sam McDonald Park, CA

I got out of the car at the trailhead and stretched, inhaling deeply to absorb as much of the intoxicating redwood aroma as possible. I heard a blue jay call, and my eyes scanned the treetops looking for it. As I did, I noticed the patches of misty sky amidst the towering canopy. The sky was still gray, but it was no longer raining. Showers and ocean mist are quite common in this forest, and consequently, the moss, ferns, shamrocks, bushes, and redwoods are always green.

I walked to the small building by the parking lot; no one was in the office. I filled out the park use envelope with my information and tucked money inside. Then I tore off the stub and dropped the envelope in the slot and put the stub on my dashboard.

I started up the trail. The beginning is a strenuous climb, but from there the trail gets easier, despite the up-and-down terrain. I paused. I could hear water running and I looked for a stream. It was partially hidden by undergrowth as it softly trickled over the rocks and down the hill. Hearing this gentle sound and thinking about the journey this water made to the ocean reminded me how much I missed being in these woods.

Trees Entwined in Mist
Redwood Forest, CA

This forest has many banana slugs, which are bright yellow, banana-shaped, slimy mollusks that can grow up to ten inches long. They have two large tentacles on the top of their heads that help them see and sense their surroundings. Their bright color makes them easy to spot among the fallen leaves and pine needles, and since they help decompose decaying matter, they are well-suited to this environment. On each of my hikes, I count the banana slugs, and on this day, I counted 36.

Their greatest protection is they produce an anesthetic that makes their predator's tongue and throat numb; this also applies to humans. If you put your tongue on a banana slug, its mucus coating will deaden your tongue. I can't speak from experience about this, but my grandson assured me it was true. Just know that touching or *kissing* a slug can be harmful to them and uncomfortable for you. My granddaughter's take on the matter was, "It just seems gross." I had to agree.

Yellow Banana Slug

By the time I had hiked most of the trail, I arrived at the campfire circle. This spot has a long bench hewn out of a giant log with smaller round logs arranged beside it to form a circle for seating. This is a favorite spot and one reason I love this trail. I always pause here to enjoy nature and write in my journal.

Knowing the bench would be wet, I came prepared with a piece of plastic to sit upon. I pulled it out of my backpack and placed it on the bench. I also had a blanket to wrap myself in because I get chilled as I rest and my body cools down. I got comfortable and removed my journal from my pack.

I observed my surroundings and then began writing. I stopped periodically to gather my thoughts and listen to the moisture dripping from the trees. Rarely are birds seen or heard this deep in the forest, and the only sound is the breeze swaying the treetops. I searched the ground for newts, which are salamanders that inhabit this area. Unlike the banana slugs, they are hard to spot, because they blend with the fallen twigs and pine needles. I found two.

After I had rested and recorded my thoughts, I put the journal back in my bag; I was finished there. I packed up my things and walked the rest of the loop to my car.

I had worked up an appetite, so I stopped in Half Moon Bay for a much-anticipated seafood dinner. It appeared the Chart House, which had been my favorite restaurant, was closed, so I checked some Yelp reviews and chose the Miramar Beach Restaurant. It was early, but I still had a couple of hours of drive time to Lawson's Landing, where I would camp for two nights.

The restaurant had an expansive view of the ocean, and its menu included Sole Dore. I had been craving fresh-caught sole for months, so was thrilled to see it listed. After a splendid meal in this scenic spot, I continued up the coast.

It had been many years since I camped in Lawson's Landing campground at Dillon Beach, but I still had fond memories of being there. Back then, there were rows of trailer homes at the back end of the park. The only campground improvements were a few picnic tables, water spigots, and porta-potties that were scattered throughout the area.

No sites were marked; you could claim as much area for your camp as you wanted. People strung yellow tape to mark their space. Then the barbeque grills, folding tables, chairs, kites, and frisbees came out. Few people had found this jewel, so it wasn't crowded and there were few rules.

As I drove, I remembered the weekend I took my granddaughter and two grandsons camping there. After the campfire died down, we sat on our mats in the tent, told spooky stories, and scared ourselves. We played with glow sticks, which created magical lines of light that danced around the tent.

My granddaughter had picked up a paper when we were at the grocery store in town, and on the cover, there were pictures of the winners of the Ugly Dog Contest. By flashlight, we read about them and made up stories about what it would be like to own each of them. For me, it was a magical time sharing in the fertile imaginations of little people.

Campsites marked off at Lawson's Landing
Photo from their website

Lawson's Landing has always been my go-to place for ocean-side camping. When I arrived, I stopped at the office to sign in and then drove through the campground; it had changed. The trailer houses were gone. They had marked individual spaces off for tents and RVs. The list of rules seemed to have grown, and the price reflected the passage of time.

I quickly set up camp and then climbed over the dunes to the beach. The mounds of sand that separated the campground from the ocean were still there, but they, too, had changed with the ocean winds. Thick clouds obscured the setting sun, so it was hard to tell how low in the sky it was.

Barefoot, I strolled down the beach, getting just close enough that the chilly water swirled around my feet, pulling the sand from under them. As I walked, I breathed deeply and kept my eye out for shells or sea stars. I found nothing, but the search added purpose to my walk.

I wasn't ready to leave the water, but it would be dark soon so I retraced my steps, telling myself I still had another day to enjoy the ocean.

The light was gone when my weary body crawled into the tent. I felt like a doggie that had had a big day out sniffing all the unfamiliar smells and running for miles. I curled up and slept, dreaming of all the pleasant happenings of the day.

The screeching of the seagulls scrounging for food awakened me. I lay in my cozy bed listening to them squawk, probably fighting for fish carcasses down at the docks. I thought about my day; there was nothing on my list to do except play by the water. What a luxurious thought!

I lay for a while and then emerged from the tent to fix a cup of Earl Grey tea. I sat in my lounge chair and sipped, as my mind floated high in the sky along with the children's kites fluttering in the sea breeze. This was paradise; I felt joy deep inside.

After some nourishment, I went to the beach. I walked along the water's edge and then stopped to build a sandcastle. After all the practice I had in my sandbox as a child, I was a master builder. Back then, I got water from the garden hose to wet the sand and make it stick together. Here, I could build it close enough to the water so the sand was wet, but not so close that the tide would quickly wash it away. I hadn't forgotten how to build a fine castle, and when I finished, I admired it and then wandered back down the shore to camp.

My stomach was telling me it was time for sustenance, so I made a tuna sandwich. Sitting at the table, nibbling on my lunch, I thought about nothing in particular and recorded it all in my journal. Reading it later, I was surprised by the profound thoughts I had recorded. It seemed amazing what one can come up with when the mind is relaxed.

I strolled around the campground and greeted people I passed, but I quickly realized that most of them just wanted to be left alone. They had come from the metropolitan areas to get away from people, not to meet strangers.

I walked to the docks, which had never interested me, but I had to see what my daughter was talking about when she related stories of her camping experiences here. Once she learned that crabbing was plentiful in this area, she caught the Dillon Beach fever. She and her friends often came with their camping trailers to crab, along with many other crab lovers.

A Crab Pot

Live Crabs

Sadly she discovered there were crab thieves who came in the night and stole the crabbers' treasures. Some were humans who pulled the crab pots out of the water and took the crustaceans that did not belong to them, and some were bandits who robbed coolers.

She was not at all amused by those who emptied their traps, however, when the *cooler gang* plundered their ice chest, she was upset and also entertained. By the footprints surrounding the cooler, she knew the gang was a family of raccoons. It seems the crabs were fair game, and it's up to the owner to protect their bounty.

Thieves in the night never bothered me, but then I am not a crabber and always stowed food in the car. The constant 10-15 mile per hour wind was the only thing that rustled my tent.

Despite the changes over the years, Lawson's Landing has provided many fun adventures for my family and me. Camping at the ocean offers many forms of entertainment limited only by one's imagination. It is a good place to rest and unwind, possibly because the sound of wind and waves cancel out the noise in one's head, allowing people to leave their city lives behind.

My time at Lawson's Landing passed quickly, and I was grateful I had these few days to rest before the next leg of my journey, which I knew would not be easy. But it, too, was part of my walk-about and I knew I needed to have the experiences it would provide.

The Takeaway: Keep your treasures secured and check out the Ugly Dog Awards.

Story 9
Coming Home

One thing about camping is that I fall into the rhythm of the sun by going to bed early and getting up early. So I was up shortly after the sun. Following tea and a simple breakfast, I packed the car. I had a few hours of drive time to reach the couple's house where I would be staying.

On the way, I decided to go through the Bay Area. Years before, I had lived in Mountain View, and after work, I donned my Nikes and went for a run at Shoreline Park. It called to me so I stopped. I got out of the car and walked up the incline to the south end of San Francisco Bay.

Shoreline Park Mountain View, CA

The seagulls, egrets, ducks, geese, coots, and stilts called out as they paddled in the water, ran on the shore, or soared overhead. It brought back pleasant memories. After my run, I'd cool down by walking on the levee. Coming here always washed away the stress of the workday. I didn't have time to do that today, but I enjoyed the reverie. It was inspiring to be in nature and the heart of the city at the same time.

After a pause at the park, I drove east and arrived at my destination; I was greeted with warm hugs. There was a lot to do and catch up on, but then things changed. This couple was having problems, and because I wanted to help, I got entangled in them. I'm sure it is no surprise to you that this was a huge mistake on my part; it was not mine to do. Their anger turned on me and drained my energy until I felt weak and exhausted. Nothing was getting better for any of us, so my only recourse was to leave.

As you might have guessed, this turned out to be a great life lesson. Once I got away and looked at what had happened, I realized I did it to myself. I should have stayed out of their issues and trusted they would find their way through them. As the wise teacher, Pooh Bear, said, "Sometimes my greatest accomplishment is just keeping my mouth shut." I got it, and now it was time to take care of myself.

Sharing wisdom

I felt frozen inside and needed to thaw out, and what better place to do that than the desert? It would be the perfect space to heal and rejuvenate.

On the first day, I drove as far as Blythe, California, where I spent a brief night. My stomach had hurt all day, but it was now quiet, as it was too tired to complain. My ears were ringing and my body was buzzing from the hours of driving. I couldn't sleep, so after tossing and turning, I got back on the road.

I could hardly wait to get to Ajo, Arizona, which is a town 115 miles south of Phoenix. I was returning to my tiny plot in the RV park that was waiting for me. I could already feel my air bed gently cradling me, as I drifted into sleep with the sounds of coyotes howling and an occasional night hawk calling in the dark. In the desert, I slept well and was eager to get up in the morning, having nature as my wake-up call. It was a pleasant start to the day.

Waking Up in the Desert

The sun would shine, and at this time of year, the air temperature would be perfect; I could already feel it warming my bones. I'd make coffee and sit at the picnic table watching the quail dashing around seeking handouts, smiling at the javelinas (medium-size wild pigs) trotting through the park making their morning rounds, and hearing the wild donkeys braying nearby. They all contributed to the wonders of the desert morning. This was indeed my magical, healing place! I beamed, thinking of the peace that awaited me.

Javelina on its Morning Rounds

With these cherished memories playing in my head, the hours of driving went by quickly. I was exhausted when I arrived back where my journey began months earlier. I felt that I had come home because, in all reality, it was the only home I had. The friends I made in February were still camped there and they welcomed me. They had not forgotten *The Girl in the Tent*.

During my travels, I purchased the items needed to set up my camp; I had a hammer, heavy orange tent stakes, and an electrical adaptor. As I put together my camp, people stopped and greeted me with friendly words and smiles. A neighbor helped me get the stakes pounded into the rocky ground. A man who looked like

Santa Claus and traveled in a Bernie Sanders van brought me a glass of fresh-squeezed orange juice. Another couple shared their fresh avocados. I chose the right place to regroup; here I felt safe, accepted, and lacked for nothing!

Over the weeks I was there, campers invited me to visit their sites to see their RV setups. They showed me the weaving and pottery projects they had completed while I was gone. Ladies shared information regarding traveling alone. RVers are a wealth of information and they share freely. My strength came back as I basked in the sun and warm conversations.

The Bernie Sanders Van 2019 Ajo, AZ

One day, I went to the clubhouse to get my dinner from the refrigerator, and a group of campers on the back patio invited me to join them. They were seated around the picnic table drinking shots of Irish whiskey and telling stories of the desert.

They related accounts of the parties they had, the immigrants who crossed the border illegally and the

76

Border Patrol who apprehended them. There was no end to the fascinating tales they told. As they downed shot after shot, I sipped a beer ignoring their encouragement to toast with a shot.

There were stories I did not understand because they used words like *chicken* and *coyote* in ways I never heard them used. From the context, I surmised a *coyote* refers to a person who smuggles people across the border. Then they said some guy came back to town to *feed the chickens* and the Border Patrol sent a van out to pick up the Mexicans. Were there chickens to be fed or was that code for giving information to the Border Patrol?

I didn't know, and it didn't matter. I wasn't even sure the stories were true, but it was healing to laugh with people who were happy and sharing. It felt fantastic! Seeing the storytellers the next morning, I was certain my beer had been the wiser choice.

After visiting with people in the RV park, I wondered if getting a van and living their lifestyle would suit me. It wasn't the first time I had entertained that thought. I love traveling, and this was an option; however, I didn't feel it would be my future. It seemed like a good idea and I knew I would enjoy it for a while, but I know myself well enough to know that, after a time, I would want a home base. I wondered if it was doable to have both.

It would please family and friends to have me settled in a permanent home as they have always had difficulty with my traveling alone. I didn't want them to worry when *The Plan* with Curley School failed, so I told them I was on a walkabout, which in truth, was more of a drive-about. I don't think they knew what that was, but it sounded like I had a purpose and knew what I was doing. Besides, they had heard me say that before, and I had emerged unscathed, so it helped calm their fears.

I can't truthfully say I knew what I was doing, but I was definitely on a walkabout. Walkabouts are not straightforward journeys, and anything can happen. You deal with whatever comes up and continue walking. There is no destination, so you are bound to get where you are going and you are never late. This may not be comfortable, but in the end, it can be most rewarding.

I always get to where I'm going by
walking away from where I was.
The Wisdom of Pooh Bear

Since I had no plan, it was easier to stay open to possibilities, and after the last few months, a plan proved less important than it had been. I could stay in my camp space as long as I wanted, and instead of worrying about the future, I used the time to explore the desert, be with people, and just have fun.

My mantra was still the phrase I heard when I first arrived in Ajo. "Rest and the answers will come." So I did.

The Takeaway: It is important to create a safe space for ourselves, and as we rest in it, we heal.

Story 10
Teens Paint the Town

Ajo is the village of festivals! These celebrations take place throughout the year, except during the scorching summer heat. My favorite festival is the March Arts Weekend, a biennial event when young artists come from across the country and Northern Mexico to paint murals on the exterior walls of the buildings around the Plaza.

Most of the painters are teens with a vision and enthusiasm for creating works of art that will last for years and inspire thousands. It was the murals from the 2017 weekend event that attracted me to Ajo and caused me to remember this tiny town. Quite by chance, this arrival in Ajo coincided with the 2019 event. I was thrilled!

The event started on Friday when they sectioned off the walls, and each group was assigned a space. I don't know how the size and placement were determined because some were three feet square and others covered most of a wall. Scaffolding, ladders, canopies, tables, and spotlights for evening work were set in place. Gallons of paint, cans of spray paint, and brushes were put out for the muralists to use. The artists painted through the weekend, and the event ended on Sunday evening when the paintings were complete.

Twice a day, I walked to the plaza to check their progress and photograph each phase of their development. As I watched, I marveled at the painters who wore dressy clothing, thinking they must be very neat. Others dressed as I would, knowing that by the time I finished, I would be wearing the same colors as the wall. The spray artists included respirators in their attire. The teens chatted seriously amongst themselves and often broke into laughter. They appeared to be having a great time.

Artist having fun

Some artists had a drawing they consulted, but most seemed to work from an image held only in their minds. Several people worked on a painting giving the impression that they were one, as their brush strokes blended and appeared synchronized. Other teams had only one person working at a time. Observers stood around talking, while some of us recorded the event in images.

Several artists created their murals with intricate brush strokes from a palette of colors, others with large house brushes, and still others with spray cans. They all had a message, whether written in words or implied by the image. Each painting was as individual as its creators.

Artist working from a Palette

Muralist using a Palette and a Small Brush

Mural with a Spelled-Out Message

When the muralists worked in the evening, the spotlights cast shadows on the walls, adding another dimension to their work. I wondered how they could tell the true color when shadows seemed to compete for attention.

Muralist Spray Painting at Night

Along with the painting, there were community events for both the locals and visitors, including a gallery walk, town potluck, local tours, live music, a block party with dancing, and of course, viewing the new murals. It was indeed a testament to the art that was breathing life back into this once near-deserted town.

I wanted to be part of the event, so I went to the International Sonoran Desert Alliance (ISDA) office and asked how I could help. They used some of my photos on their website and put me to work serving the evening meal on Saturday. The co-sponsors, Ajo Council for the Arts and ISDA, provided hotdogs, roast pork and beef, veggie burgers, chicken, and hamburgers; the townspeople provided the side dishes. I welcomed this opportunity to contribute to the festivities, while also meeting the townspeople. Most everyone I had met up until now was from the RV park.

After I finished serving, I dished a plate for myself and took a seat at a table. As we took turns introducing ourselves, I was pleasantly surprised to learn that everyone at the table was an artisan. There was a cartoonist, jeweler, painter, photographer, and potter. Everyone had their area of interest.

As they visited, they shared information about other events taking place that weekend, like the retro-camper show by a man who restored travel trailers from the 1960s and an art show hosted by several artists. It was indeed an interesting evening and opened doors to meeting some of the full-time residents.

Feeling satiated with camaraderie and all of the information they shared, I did not stay for the street dance. I returned to my campsite, and as I lay in my tent, I could hear the music in the distance. It brought a smile to my face.

Ajo seemed to have a lot going on, and people participated, but there was something *off* that I couldn't quite identify at that time. I asked myself if I could be a permanent part of this community. I wasn't sure.

There was also the question of the summer heat which would be an issue for me. With that thought, another option popped into my head. What would happen if I bought a house to live there in the winter months and a camper van for travel in the summer? It sounded possible, and I would look into it.

But for now, all was well. I had a place to stay, and I was safe and comfortable. Nothing was going to get decided tonight. So my directive was still, "Rest and the answers will come."

The Takeaway: Tiny towns have much to offer.

Story 11
Joy Board

Although I had traveled many miles, I still had not found my new home. I was questioning why things weren't coming together and wondered if I was to travel from one place to another and sleep in my tent for the rest of my life. I was okay with that; however, that was not my first choice.

It was at this point in my journey when I stopped in Santa Fe and had lunch with my friend Lynne, who is a Reiki Master. She offered to do a session for me and I agreed. It would be nurturing to receive the universal life force energy, which feels like an energy massage. While I was on her massage table, she had the knowingness that it would be helpful for me to create an art piece to help move through any stuck energy that might be keeping me from finding my new home.

When she said this, it surprised me because my art supplies were all in storage, but I assured her I would consider her words. Without materials, I knew it couldn't be a typical art piece, and it still had to be special and reflect my journey. I thought about the ocean, the redwood forest, Biosphere II, and the other wonderful places I had experienced. The new and old friends I'd been with also came to mind and I felt the love and support I had along the way. It didn't take long to realize what my project would be.

I would make a collage of photos I had taken of the people and places that had brought me joy on my journey. There were so many! How would I choose which best represented my experiences? For hours, I sat at the picnic table going through my phone and camera to see what images I had. As I did, I relived each experience. Despite the glitches that had come up, I realized I was having the adventure of a lifetime!

I purchased an 11" x 14" black canvas, origami papers, stickers, and removable tape. At the drugstore, I printed out lots of photos. Armed with the photos and supplies, I returned to my campsite excited to create an art piece.

I placed things on the canvas, cut them, and repositioned them. When I got them where I wanted, I taped them onto the canvas and then placed the stickers on the board. The stickers said things like, "Go for it," "Believe," "Take pride in how far you have come," and "Have faith in how far you can go." I titled the piece after a phrase I had heard that spoke to me, "The Sublime Joy of Being in Experience." This would remind me to stay in joy and radiate it into my day.

I felt deep inner joy and satisfaction as I looked at the completed project and wanted it close to me so I could look at it often. And I knew exactly what I would do with it. For the rest of the trip, that canvas rode on the front seat next to me, and I took it into my tent every night. Each time I gazed at it, I smiled as I remembered the story that went with each image. I felt the same joy I felt at the moment of that experience. I called it my *Joy Board*.

I didn't consider until much later that my Joy Board was the reverse of a *Vision Board*. To make a Vision Board, you post pictures of things you want but don't yet have. These images were not things I was asking for, but things I was feeling grateful for already having. They were pictures of my past and also of my future because, as I expressed appreciation for these people, events, and experiences, the joy I felt brought more magic into my days.

My Joy Board

My Joy Board did its magic to keep me in a state of pure delight, reminding me that everything was an experience to be treasured. Sure, there were bumps in the road, but every bump was far outweighed by the many blessings and good times. And it was good to have the reminder.

The Takeaway: Having gratitude for what we have opens the door for more good things to come.

Story 12
The Fast

When Lynne offered to do the Reiki session, it was truly the perfect gift for that moment. In the past, I had trouble receiving, but I was different now and graciously accepted her offer. Her kindness brought back a memory of a camping experience in the Bighorn Mountains during the time I was unable to ask for or receive help.

On that camping trip, I wanted to enhance the period of introspection in nature by doing a lemon juice cleanse. This is a fast that consists of eating nothing and drinking only a concoction of lemon juice, maple syrup, water, and a dash of cayenne pepper.

Over the years, I had done this fast for three days, seven days, and often extended it to ten days, so I assumed a few days would be easy. On this trip, I did not bring food, but instead, lots of lemons, maple syrup, and a bottle of cayenne pepper. Since there were no grocery stores for miles, I knew I would stick to the regimen.

I was younger then, and I pushed my body hard. It seemed like a good idea, and it probably would have worked just fine, if it had not been for the springtime pollen and my allergy to it. The tiny particles of golden dust filled the air.

As I was setting up camp, I started sneezing and could not stop. Then my nose ran as if someone had turned a spigot on. My symptoms quickly escalated until my heart raced and felt it would never beat properly again. I hurried to get the tent up and my bed made, so I could get inside where I hoped I'd have some protection from the pollen.

The other campers were staring, so as soon as my shelter was up, I slipped into it where I didn't have to witness their concerned looks. As a small child, I learned that if I couldn't see people, they couldn't see or hear me either. I guess I still naively believed that to some extent.

The sneezing did not stop; in fact, it got progressively worse. Exhausted, I lay down, but that didn't help; my heart continued its frantic pounding. After using half the box of Kleenex, which is no exaggeration, I went to the car in search of allergy medication. I returned to my tent and sat holding the box of meds, knowing this would not have a pleasant ending.

I had not eaten, so my stomach was empty, and after a fast, I always slowly reintroduced food back into the body, beginning with orange juice. It would not like me putting anything, especially drugs, into it but I didn't know what other choice I had. I couldn't continue this blowing and sneezing. From experience, I knew once these symptoms started, the sinus membranes became so irritated that they would not stop reacting without the help of an antihistamine.

If only I had something to help buffer my stomach from the medication. It never occurred to me to ask a fellow camper if they had something they would share with me, plus they would not have liked me sneezing all over them as I tried to explain what I needed. I didn't ask for help, and if they had offered it, I probably would have been too embarrassed to accept it. This may sound silly, but that's how I was back then, plus I was not thinking clearly.

[NOTE: Today, while writing this, I realized I could have had an extra dose of water with maple syrup in it, which would have given my stomach some protection.]

Reluctantly, I took the recommended dose of medication. Within minutes, my stomach felt like a grenade had gone off. Now added to the sneezing, I was also vomiting. It was good I had my *honey pot* close by.

At this point, I debated going to the campground hosts for help, but there was nothing they could do. I just had to ride it out. I had visions of them finding my body the next day, surrounded by used Kleenex and a bucket of stomach lining, wondering what had happened. Eventually, the sneezing, nose-blowing, and rapid heart rate subsided, but the stomachache continued into the night.

The next morning, I was surprised when I woke up; I had made it through the night! Weak and exhausted, I packed up and went home. The retreat and cleanse

I was looking to do turned into a bigger event than I had anticipated. While it was not my vision of how this time would go, I returned home feeling I was flushed out from top to bottom.

This was a profound experience, but I would not recommend it, nor would I ever do it again.

The Takeaway: Be prepared and ask for help when needed.

Story 13
The Bosque

After I left Santa Fe, I felt rejuvenated. The talk with Lynne and the Reiki she shared helped me get back on track. I am used to taking care of myself, but it was nice to have this boost of support.

I wanted to visit the Bosque del Apache National Wildlife Refuge in southern New Mexico, so as I headed south on Interstate 25, I decided there was no time like the present to go. Most of the large birds would have left the refuge to return north, and it would take me a few miles out of the way, but no matter; I had the time.

Bosque is a Spanish word that means *woodlands found along river banks*. Bosque del Apache means *woods of the Apache*, named for the Apache tribes that once camped there. It is about 53,000 acres and is only one of many bosques in the southwestern United States.

Water flowing through the Bosque

Many bird species migrate to this refuge to spend the winter. The numbers vary, but there are estimates of 14,000 sandhill cranes and 32,000 snow geese that travel from their summer homes in Canada and eastern Siberia to winter there. Between November and February, they become the major attraction for birders and photographers who gather from all parts of the United States to witness, film, and take part in this event.

Snow Geese, Bosque del Apache, NM

I went to the visitor's center and found that, despite the large birds having flown back north, many smaller ones remained. A window in the center had feeders that attracted various species and provided an excellent place for viewing. After watching the birds and looking at the exhibits, one of the volunteers invited me outside to the gardens they had planted to display specimens of the native plants. One of the most unusual things he showed me was the seed from screwbean mesquite. It is a small shrub different from the traditional mesquite, because of its corkscrew-shaped bean pods that appear in the summer.

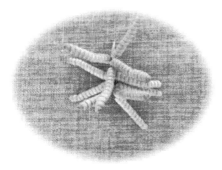

Screwbean Mesquite Pod

After we finished the tour, I drove through the north and south loops of the refuge and hiked two of the many trails to see birds that were not interested in the feeders at the building. They preferred the ponds and the grain left in the surrounding fields.

This oasis feels like a place out of time, and the rest of the world fades when I am there. It is a beautiful and fragile wetland in the Land of Enchantment's high desert. It is a section of the Rio Grande River that operates much as it has historically, but now it requires management to keep it viable for wildlife. The biggest issue is that the river does not have the water flow it once did.

I did not see the sandhill cranes and snow geese on this trip, but I spotted a roadrunner, a herd of six javelinas (medium-sized wild pigs), turtles sunning themselves on half-sunken rocks and logs, a blue heron, several mule deer, hawks, many mallards, and a few bufflehead ducks.

Blue Heron and Turtle in a Face-off

I have always thought the wood duck is the prettiest of the duck species but, after I saw the buffleheads, it is a toss-up between the two. These small beauties have a white body, a black back and head, and a large white patch around the back of their head. Their unusual name is derived from buffalo-head for the male's puffy head shape. They are North America's smallest diving ducks and glide through the water, barely leaving a wake behind them.

Bufflehead Duck, Bosque del Apache, NM

On another trip to the Bosque, I timed it to be there when the sandhill cranes and snow geese were present. The event that excites most people takes place at sunrise when thousands of geese take off *en masse* to feed in the fields of the Rio Grande Valley. Just after sunrise, the cranes leave the ponds in smaller groups to forage in the surrounding fields. I have seen pictures of this *fly-out* and thought it was something to encounter, but since I am not one to get up and out in the cold before sunrise, I have, instead, opted to be there at dusk for their return to the ponds.

Sandhill Cranes at Dusk, Bosque del Apache

The geese slowly return to the wetlands before dark. The cranes return as the sun is setting. It is quite impressive to watch as they fly back to the ponds in a steady stream. It takes about an hour for them to return to the safety of the water.

The most outstanding thing is that their calls can be heard over two miles away, and as they get closer, they drown out all other sounds, including any conversation you may be having. The cranes give loud, rattling bugle calls lasting a couple of seconds, although they seem to last longer when strung together. These calls are a communication system that keeps families together and signals if danger is present.

I have returned to the Bosque del Apache many times because, no matter what time of year, it is one of the most peaceful places I have experienced. I drive the loops at leisure, stop at the viewing areas, and hike the trails. It is a wonderful place to take a break and get in touch with nature. And I always come home with new photos of the wildlife.

The Takeaway: Whether you are a morning or evening person, the Bosque del Apache provides one of the most spectacular events nature offers.

Story 14
Route 66

After the Bosque, I drove Interstate 25 north to Interstate 40 east. Driving I-40 is always fun because it follows the historic Route 66 through Texas, New Mexico, Arizona, and California. Many remnants of this iconic highway are still in existence, and because it has been so enjoyable for me, I have made it the subject of this Story.

In the early 1960s, there was a television program called "Route 66." The episodes took two young friends, Tod Stiles and Buz Murdock, across the country in their Chevrolet Corvette convertible. Tod was from a wealthy family that lost its fortune, and Buz was from the streets of New York. On their travels, they worked various jobs and met interesting people. They had romantic, dangerous, and exciting escapades.

I watched this show every week, and although many episodes did not take place on Route 66, I came to see this iconic trans-American highway as one possessing grand adventure. As they drew me into their dramas, I dreamed of driving Route 66 in a convertible, but mine would not be a Corvette, it would be a Ford Thunderbird.

Over the years, I have followed my dream and have driven the remaining stretches of Route 66 from

Texas to California and dipped into the history of the Southwest, but I did it in a sedan, not a convertible.

Route 66 was constructed in the 1920s with the last segment being completed in 1926. It was one of the first highways in the U.S. highway system. This road was important because it served as the first all-weather highway and shortened the driving distance from Chicago, Illinois, to Santa Monica, California, by 200 miles.

Original U.S. Route 66 Signage

This may not seem like a great distance to us with vehicles that travel 70-80 miles per hour and the outstanding four-lane highways we have. But in the early 1900s, cars averaged 50 miles per hour, and the roads were difficult to travel, so this highway could save travelers many hours.

During the dustbowl days of the 1930s, Route 66 became known as the *Mother Road* because it symbolized hope. Drought and dust storms damaged the crops in the Midwest and destroyed people's livelihoods. They left their homes and traveled the Mother Road to California in search of jobs and a better life. Later on, it was called *America's Mainstreet* because it connected so many states and small towns.

When the interstate road system was built, Route 66 became obsolete and was decommissioned in 1985 after 59 years of service. It is estimated that 85% is still drivable, but only fragments are marked with the Historic Route 66 signage.

Signs that now mark Route 66

I have made many trips between Santa Fe and California, and I always stop someplace on Route 66, but I had not explored the highway to the east. After leaving the Bosque del Apache, I had time to take a side trip to the section of Route 66 by Amarillo, Texas, to visit Cadillac Ranch.

Cadillac Ranch is an outdoor public art installation that was built in 1974. It has ten very colorful fat-fender Cadillacs buried nose-first in the ground. The Caddies range from 1949 to 1963. Over the years, people have placed so much graffiti on the cars that the paint is inches thick and peels off in chunks. It is fun to take a can or two of spray paint and share a message with those who will follow.

Cadillac Ranch, Amarillo, TX

Cadillac Ranch, Amarillo, Texas

I picked up pieces of paint from the ground and created a photo collage honoring this historic piece of art. I later donated it to the Route 66 Auto Museum in Santa Rosa, New Mexico. If you are ever driving through that area and need a break, stop by this fun museum and see the piece I made for them.

Donated *Art Collage*
Route 66 Auto Museum, Santa Rosa, NM

When I left Amarillo, I drove 35 miles to Slug Bug Ranch in Conway, Texas. I had to see the poor man's version of Cadillac Ranch. It is called Slug Bug Ranch because it has five Volkswagen Beetles buried nose-deep in the ground. People have also covered these cars with graffiti. I have been to Cadillac and Slug Bug Ranches twice, and each time, the cars look different because the artists and messages change.

Slug Bug Ranch, Conway, TX

Slug Bug Ranch has an old abandoned car and a shed that are also painted. This is where I was introduced to *Live a Great Story* by a sticker that was posted on the very colorful antique car. I didn't realize the significance of this sticker, but I thought it was an amazing sentiment that summed up my life's purpose.

Later, when I Googled it, I found it was an inspirational movement started by Zach Horvath. He had the one simple thought that every person has the power to share their story, and by doing so, they become an inspiration to others.

Unknowingly, he started the movement when he sprayed his message in red paint on a wall in Austin, Texas. People saw it and began sharing pictures on social media with their personal and inspired responses, and soon there was a movement called *Live a Great Story*.

Live a Great Story by Zach Horvath

The Ranches were fun to visit, and I have used my photos in various art projects, which remind me of the entertaining times I had there. As I have said, Route 66 holds a special place in my heart, and these bits of roadside Americana are part of the reason.

Route 66 through Albuquerque, New Mexico, has a display of neon lights that were popular during the early to mid-1900s. But the most cherished relic was in Tijeras just east of Albuquerque. It was a segment of Route 66 that caused me to feel like an excited child when I drove on it.

It was called *The Musical Highway*. It was a quarter-mile section of road that, if you drove 45 miles per hour, the rumble bars sang *America the Beautiful*. I drove over it again and again, as I couldn't believe how precise it was. You really could hear the song being played by the tires hitting the concrete strips along the edge of the road.

Recently, my daughter came to visit, and I took her to experience it, but they had paved over it! I almost cried; it was such a marvelous work of art. Thankfully, it has been preserved in videos on YouTube.com.

Wigwam Motel, Holbrook, Arizona

There are many fascinating things to experience on Route 66, but two towns that cause many people to stop are Holbrook and Winslow, Arizona. Holbrook is famous for the Wigwam Motel where you can sleep in a concrete tipi. Mr. Maestas café is not to be missed. It is on the left as you drive into town and is full of memorabilia—some you might recognize from your grandmother's house, or perhaps your childhood home. There is much to explore at the museum, which is supposedly haunted. The Bucket of Blood Saloon where the fights were so bloody that the cleanup required a bucket is now in ruins. And of course, the Painted Desert is a must-see with all of its colors and petrified wood.

The Wigwam Motel and the Painted Desert are honored in the animated movie *Cars*. The tow trucks scattered around town are immortalized by the lovable *Cars* character *Mater*. Interestingly, the main car, *Lightning McQueen*, was a combination of several things. They began with a Corvette and made changes so it looked more dynamic. I have wondered if the people at Pixar Animation Studios had the Corvette from the television series *Route 66* in mind when they designed Lightning McQueen.

One of the Rusted Tow Trucks, Holbrook, AZ

The abandoned, rusted tow trucks are witness to the many vehicles that broke down in the 100-plus degree desert heat. These tow trucks were indeed a blessing to travelers crossing this desolate land. One can only imagine riding in a car with no air conditioning and having the engine overheat. In those days, cars frequently broke down because of extreme temperatures, and there were no cell phones to call for help. Not happy thoughts!

Thirty miles from Holbrook is Winslow, Arizona. This town doesn't have as many relics from the past, but it does have the beautiful La Posada Hotel, complete with a restaurant and art gallery. The town's major attraction, however, is the iconic rock and roll Standin' on the Corner in Winslow, Arizona Park.

La Posada Hotel, Winslow, AZ

La Posada Hotel Portal, Winslow, AZ

Standing on the Corner is a line from the song *Take It Easy*. In the small park, there are two statues paying tribute to the composers of the song, Jackson Browne and Glenn Frey. There is an eagle on the roof of the building acknowledging the Eagles who sang the song. There is also a mural in the window that depicts the line from the song "It's a girl, my Lord, in a flatbed Ford slowin' down to take a look at me."

The Standin' on the Corner Park attracts 100,000 people each year who photograph this piece of Americana and have their pictures taken with an arm around the statues. Much of the interest is because of the Eagles, who were extremely popular in the 1970s. Their *Greatest Hits* album was the best-selling album of the 20th century in the U.S., and they sold more records than any American band in the 1970s. People loved them because "their songs were a soundtrack to our lives."

Bikers Riding by Standin' on the Corner Park

I suspect those who stop at this site are people who love the Eagles and want to relive a bit of the past. Just being there, you can feel the nostalgia for what seemed like a simpler time.

Standin' on the Corner in Winslow, AZ

There are more things to explore on Route 66, as it continues through California. For instance, San Bernardino has a Wigwam Motel and is the home of the first McDonald's hamburger stand. Victorville supports a Route 66 Museum. The end of the trail for Route 66 is the Pacific Ocean at the Santa Monica pier in California, where one can enjoy moderate temperatures and the sun 310 days out of the year.

Besides making the trip more interesting, Route 66 provides stops that break up the drive across the long stretches of desert. Wherever I have stopped on this historic highway, I have seen something that brings a smile and puts a song in my heart.

The Takeaway: "Get your kicks on Route 66".

Story 15
Farewell to an Old Friend

While waiting for my breakfast in Holbrook's Mr. Maestas café on Route 66, I looked around at all the memorabilia (junk to some) and thought about how I got started camping on my own. It began in the mid-1990s.

I worked as a server at a restaurant in Keystone, South Dakota, which is a popular tourist town at the foot of Mt. Rushmore. I took the job because I thought it would be fun to meet people from other places, and I could use the money. It was too far to drive home at night, so I stayed in the dorm with my co-workers.

The other bunks were occupied by people who wanted to party. My partying days were long gone, and after being on my feet all day, all I wanted was to sleep. Between the smell of alcohol and cigarette smoke, the loud talking, and the music, I could not rest. There was no sleep to be had in the dorm, so I went to the lake, curled up in a blanket at the water's edge, and slept. It was peaceful, and I rested well, but this was not a long-term solution. I was not sure what I was going to do.

My family was getting together in a town not far away, so on my day off, I drove over and joined them. As we talked, my story came out, and to give me another option, my brother went to his garage and pulled out a tent. It was twenty years old and had been passed from one family member to another. He also handed me a sleeping bag. Both were in good condition, though not the latest style and fabric. I was grateful and graciously accepted both.

I went back to work, and after being with people who loved and respected me, I realized that job was abuse on all levels. Even though I was paying for my accommodations, I was not getting any sleep. I had witnessed another server stealing tips from my tables. And the last blow came during our downtime when the managers had me clean and restock while they and their favorite employees sat around smoking and laughing. Enough! I was not Cinderella. It was time to quit. And at that very moment, I did!

I drove back to the ranch in Wanblee, South Dakota, where I lived. The way things turned out, I didn't need my new camping equipment then, but now that I had a tent and a sleeping bag, I knew I would use them.

That is how I acquired the tent that was to become my traveling buddy. It was nylon and shaped like a little six-sided dome. It was originally forest green but had faded to brown on top and army green at the base. I loved that tent and we traveled together for twenty years. I spent many nights sleeping in the shelter she provided.

By the time she reached forty years old, she was showing her age. She had a few tiny pinholes in the nylon. The zipper on one of the flaps was broken, and I had patched it together with safety pins. At one time, I could set it up in five minutes, no joke!

Dome Tent Without Rain Fly

However, the older she got, the longer it took as the elastic bands in the rods broke, and I had to piece the plastic spines together and hold them in place as I ran them through the fabric loops. Some of them had also split like green sticks, and that didn't help. I tried to replace the plastic parts, but they were no longer available, so I dealt with the situation as best I could. Yes, she had her little quirks, but we had been through wind, rain, ice, and hail together; she always sheltered me and kept me dry. We had history!

For Christmas one year, I received a new tent, and for a while, I continued to sleep in my old one but carried the new one as a backup should I need it. I couldn't bring myself to replace my tried-and-true friend with a younger model. The new shelter was much bigger and would not have the cozy feeling my little dome had. I resisted transitioning, but I finally conceded that she had served well for 40 years, and now it was time to let her go.

Without change, there would be no butterflies.
Holiday in the Wild

It was time for a change, but I couldn't just throw her in the trash after all the experiences we had shared, so I considered holding a burial ceremony. I wrote an ode to her, and on my travels, I looked for her perfect resting place.

While driving across the Southwest, my eye was drawn to a huge mound. It looked like soft soil that would be easy to dig a hole in. I exited the highway and drove to it. I stopped the car, got out my camping spade, and started shoveling. It wasn't as easy to move the dirt as I originally thought it would be, but I got a proper hole ready.

Near the Burial Site

I gently placed her and the plastic pieces in their final resting place. To the tune of Auld Lang Sine, I sang the ode I had written and then placed the poem in the grave with her. Tears streamed down my cheeks; this was indeed a sad day! Not only did I lose a trusted buddy, but I now had to build a relationship with the unfamiliar tent. I resented having to make the change, as I knew this tent would be more difficult to set up. Later, I found this to be true, especially in the rain. We will talk about that in another Story.

This may sound like crackers to you, but I traveled alone, and without reliable equipment, it could have been a nightmare. The tent was doing what she was manufactured to do, but she was truly a gift and served me well.

I have learned that when I treat my car, home, and belongings with respect, they remain in good condition and serve me well beyond their expected life span.

The Takeaway: Appreciate the things that serve you, and see what the results are.

Story 16
The Ancient Wheel

As promised, we will now talk about my first experience setting up the new tent. I have made pilgrimages to many sacred sites, and one of my favorite places is the ancient Medicine Wheel in the Bighorn National Forest. Throughout the years, the Indigenous People have built many of these stone structures across the country.

They resemble a wagon wheel, having a center pile of stones surrounded by lines of rocks, like spokes, going out to an outer ring of stones. They are often constructed on the summit of a hill and can be of different sizes. This Medicine Wheel is 80 feet in diameter, has 28 spokes, and sits 9642 feet above sea level. It is located off U.S. Highway 14A east of Lovell, Wyoming. Because of heavy snow, the facility is only open from mid-June to mid-September.

Ancient Medicine Wheel, Wyoming

The first time I went to this area, I arrived at night because I got a late start leaving South Dakota. I wasn't concerned about having to set up camp in the dark; it would not be the first time I had pitched my tent by light from the car headlamps. However, I hadn't counted on rain—torrential, non-stop rain!

The other thing I had not considered was that I had a new tent, and it was constructed differently from my previous one. To put it together, I had to read directions, which was difficult as they became soaked with rain. It was a ten-foot square with mesh sidewalls, and the mesh was anything but waterproof. It was not until I had it pitched and the rainfly on that it was anywhere near waterproof. By the time I had the tent erected, there was an inch of water on the floor.

I thought about sleeping in the car, but I had tossed gear around inside as I scrambled to get what I needed for the night. As I did so, water got into the car. Did I mention this was a torrential downpour?

I wiped up the tent floor as best I could and put my four-inch foam mat down, hoping any remaining water would not soak through. I also wasn't sure how waterproof the tent was or if it would leak. But I had done what I could; there was nothing else to do, and worrying was not changing anything. If I got wet, I would simply go to the car and hope for the best. I crawled into my makeshift bed and relinquished control of the situation. I went into a deep sleep.

When I awoke in the morning, the rain had stopped, and the birds were singing. This campground was well over 9000 feet in elevation, so it was a brisk morning. The air was moist when I crawled out of the tent. I was dry, but most everything else was wet. I laid the mat and other wet items on the picnic table in the sun, hoping they would dry. Later, I would deal with the rest of the mess. I skipped breakfast and drove to the Medicine Wheel.

From the campground, I could see the mountain where the wheel is located high above, but to get there, I had to drive up the switchbacks. I arrived at the parking lot and began reading signs the U.S. Forest Service had posted.

I learned that this National Historic Landmark is a major Native American sacred complex and archaeological site that many tribes have used for centuries. Exactly how old the Wheel is has been debated. Some date it at a few hundred years, while others say it could be 3000 years old. Oral histories indicate it has been there for generations. Let's just say it is old!

It was a mile-and-a-half walk from where I stood to reach the Medicine Wheel. That didn't seem very far; I hiked all the time. After using the restroom, I filled my backpack with tobacco for an offering, a water bottle, my journal, blanket, camera, snacks, plus a few other things I thought I might need. I began the hike up the vertical mountain road. The high altitude and extremely steep slope made it difficult to breathe. I had to stop several times, which was okay, as it allowed me to look around.

My attention was drawn to some noisy marmots running in and out of holes in a rock mound beside the road. They seemed very busy, although it was not apparent what their mission was. Passersby did not frighten these large, squirrel-looking critters, or else their chirping would have changed to a trill or sounded like a human scream. They are primarily herbivores and will not attack a person, but the diseases they carry, like Lyme disease, Rocky Mountain spotted fever, or rabies, can be harmful.

Marmot

Marmots have long thick fur that makes them well-suited to living in cold environments. They have fur-covered ears, short, stocky legs, and strong claws for digging. They live in groups and are only active in the summer as they hibernate through the winter. When they venture from their dens, they are prey for large birds, coyotes, and bobcats. Their primary defense is they can run very fast when they sense danger.

As I wheezed my way up the mountain, a few people drove by in cars. The ranger who was stationed by the parking area had issued them a permit because they had health challenges. If someone had stopped and offered me a ride, I debated if I would take it. I wasn't sure because, even though I was feeling the exertion, there was something righteous about walking. Besides, I was here on a pilgrimage and wanted the full experience, so I continued to huff and puff my way up the mountain, stopping now and then for a drink of water and to view the surrounding mountains. I guess I appeared to be doing okay because nobody slowed down to offer a ride.

One had to take precautions with over-exertion because there were no cell towers or landline phones. The rangers didn't even have phones; they used walkie-talkies. While they could summon help, it would take time to arrive, so it was best that people came prepared and took safeguards. This may have changed over time, but the only phone I found in the remote areas of the Bighorns was a satellite phone at a resort with a price of $5.00 a minute for usage.

On this beautiful spring day, the sun was shining; the air was fresh, and the bright blue sky was without clouds. There wasn't much oxygen, but I did okay considering the elevation was 6500 feet higher than I was used to. Despite my body feeling the strain, I walked with a song in my heart. I could feel the sacredness of the land and its history. It was as if I was walking to do a ceremony with my people. Was it my imagination, or was I tapping into a memory held in the land for hundreds of years?

When I reached the peak, my reward was a 360-degree view of the distant, snow-capped mountains and the tree-covered valley below. The Medicine Wheel was to my left on a slight incline. Since the circle is a sacred site, there are protocols to follow, and rangers are present to enforce them. Some of the rules are:

- Only circle from the left. I wondered if this included the Lakota Heyoka person who does everything backward.
- Leave no prayer ties or food offerings unless you are Native American.
- Do not take anything from the area.
- Do not go inside the fenced area.

In the past, there weren't rangers or rules, but things have changed over the years after people defaced the site and removed rocks. Rock removal was one reason why cars needed a permit to drive to the circle. It is good that the Forest Service protects the site, but it felt strange having the rangers watching me.

Close by the Medicine Wheel, there was a small rock, and I took off my backpack and dropped it. From my pack, I withdrew the package of Bugler tobacco I had purchased for this occasion and put it in my pocket. Bugler is not the best tobacco, but it was all I could find. I took a handful and put the package back in my pocket.

I enjoyed doing ceremonies, and while I was hiking up the mountain, I created one in my mind that I would perform. I would walk around the circle three times, each time with a different intention.

The rules said nothing about dispersing tobacco, so I stood at the entrance holding the tobacco and declared my intention for my first circling; I would clear my past. I began walking and releasing tobacco into the air, while repeating my intention to let go of anything holding me back in life, like limiting beliefs and emotions. If they were not helping me have a better life experience, they had to go.

After I completed that round, I again filled my hand with tobacco and paused at the entrance. My aim for my second circling concerned the present. I walked, dispersed tobacco, and focused on today. I intended to be fully present with my experiences and expressed gratitude for everything in my life.

Before the third circling, I again set my goal. This time it concerned the future. I stated that I would have clarity from now on and asked to see possibilities that would enrich my life experience. I called to me whatever I needed for this to happen. As I walked, I released the tobacco offering into the breeze.

Each time I circled the Wheel, my meditation changed. I could feel the weight lifting from me, the peace of being truly present, and the excitement for my life's new potential. It was a real and impactful experience.

When I finished at the Medicine Wheel, I walked to a huge stone outcropping not far away. I pulled the blanket from my pack, unfolded it, and sat down. Even with the padding the blanket provided, the rock was bumpy and hurt my bottom, so I pretended I was Gumby and relaxed around the bumps. I stared out over the land as I ate a granola bar and drank my water.

There was a trail that went past the porta-potty, and I assumed backcountry campers used that path. I thought maybe someday I would follow it, but not to-day. The view of the surrounding mountains was expansive, green, and lush. It was awe-inspiring, and I just wanted to soak it in before I began my hike back down the mountain.

After recording my thoughts and the day's experiences in my journal, I repacked my bag and started down the road I had climbed up a few hours earlier. It was worth the effort. I felt inspired and blessed being on this land, and this feeling caused me to return to this area many times.

The Takeaway: Sometimes it is best not to know before we start something how hard it will be. That way, we take one step at a time, dealing with what comes, all the while getting closer to our goal.

Story 17
Max

Camping trips to the Bighorns became an annual event, and each time I was there, I went to the Medicine Wheel. It was a special place for me, as it is for so many others. My pilgrimage up the steep hill, the expansive views, and the sacredness of the area always left me feeling inspired.

Although I returned many times, I never camped in the Medicine Wheel campground after my experience with torrential rain and soaked equipment; that time was better left in the dark recesses of my brain. I chose not to relive it or allow it to color my enjoyment of future camping trips.

There are many campgrounds in the Bighorn National Forest, so on my next trip, I drove through one after another, looking for my perfect space. There were many places I considered, but I found *mine* in Sitting Bull Campground.

Welcome to Sitting Bull Campground

Sitting Bull Campground is on Highway 16 and sits at an elevation of 8600 feet. That is only 600 feet lower than the campground by the Medicine Wheel, but I found in the mountains a few hundred feet can make a big difference, as well as the time of year. A ranger once told me September is the best month, but I doubt he had ever tent-camped there at that time of year! I'll save that adventure for another Story. From my experience, July and August have the most favorable weather for tenting in these mountains.

As I drove into the campground, I noticed the host's fifth wheel in the first spot on the left, and next to it, the bear-proof trash receptacles and a stack of firewood for purchase. I always note the host's location in case I need their help at some point. I can't say if it is always the case, but in national forests, the hosts seem to be in the first space on the left.

On my right, I noticed a vehicle that had a tent on top of it. It looked interesting, but I wondered what the advantage was. I couldn't think of any but decided the owners probably liked the novelty of it.

I drove around the loops looking at the sites. There are a lot of things to consider before committing to a spot. I ask myself these questions. Where is the water? Where is the restroom? I knew from experience that I wanted a site close to the restroom, yet not too close. Which RVs have their generators running? Where are the dogs and children? What time of day will the sun hit my spot?

I checked all the items off my list when I reached a site at the end of one loop. It overlooked a meadow that was covered with clover and other wildflowers that looked and smelled like paradise. The 13,000-foot, snow-capped mountains beyond the field created a majestic backdrop. On this site, there were several flat places to pitch a tent; I could choose under the pine trees or in the sun. A pickup camper was in the space next to mine, so the noise would be minimal. This was the perfect spot, and I returned here on many future camping trips.

For a few days each year, I love being in nature and away from the city. In most of the national parks, there are no cell towers, electricity, or other signs of the city, unless you consider recreational vehicles with generators. The only available water is pumped from the ground. There are pit toilets, which are an updated version of an outhouse, and there is usually a bottle of hand sanitizer hanging on the wall. It is rustic to be sure.

I needed little to be comfortable; as long as I had a soft bed and was warm, life was good. My mountain camping trips were about getting out of the city and spending my time reading, writing in my journal, and sipping tea while staring into space. Purchasing an armload of wood and building a campfire, walking down ATV paths in the woods, and driving through the mountains to explore my surroundings were also my favorite activities.

Looking out over the vistas, these mountains remind me of the Grand Canyon, in that everything is so vast it is hard to estimate distance. The Bighorn National Forest is over one million acres, and the summits reach 13,000 feet. That is 3,000 feet above the tree line, so the peaks are barren unless shrouded in snow. The lower elevations are covered with lodgepole pine, fir, spruce, grasses, and wildflowers.

On my drives through the area, I have seen what appeared to be geology classes examining the rock formations alongside the road. Posted signs tell the age and period of the different rocks. One sign might say an area is 70 million years old, while further down the road, another may read 45 million. When things get that old, most people drive by and say, "Wow! That's old." The age doesn't mean much to anyone except geologists, who find it fascinating because they understand its significance. But even for a novice, it is interesting to think that the crest of the Bighorns contains rocks that are 3.25 billion years old, making it the oldest exposed rock in the world.

After one of my outings, I returned to camp in the early evening. As I turned off the highway onto the gravel that led into the campground, I saw a moose standing in the bracken about 100 yards from the road. His massive dark brown body, rounded snout, huge flat antlers, and humped back made this majestic being stand apart from the surrounding brush, which was shoulder-high on him.

Moose stand up to six feet tall at the shoulders. They have disproportionately long legs, which help them when walking through snow or deep water. Females do not have antlers, but males have ones that are velvet-covered and measure about six feet across. Testosterone, nutrition, age, and genetics regulate the size of their antlers. They shed them in late fall or early winter after the rutting season. Wild animals, like squirrels, opossums, coyotes, and bears eat the fallen antlers, as they are an excellent source of calcium, phosphorus, protein, and other nutrients.

I turned off the ignition and sat gazing in awe at this magnificent creature. We stared at each other. He showed no sign of feeling threatened; he just stood there. I suspected this had to do with the distance between us, but I knew he could kick the snot out of me if he wanted. I was sure he also knew that. Whatever the reason, I loved seeing him in the field and making eye contact with him.

I watched for a while and then went to my camp to have dinner. Seeing *Max* the moose was the highlight of my day. During my stay at the campground, I walked down the gravel road every evening to check on him, and he was always there in the same spot at the same time. It felt like I was visiting an old friend.

After seeing Max, I bought an armload of wood from the campground host and built a fire in the pit provided by the forest service. I stared into the fire and let my mind wander.

My Camp Fire

I thought about Max and moose in general. They are solitary animals, except during mating season, and I wondered about Max. Did he fight for a herd? Was he too small? He looked pretty big to me! Since I had never been in that area during rutting season, I had no idea. I just know that every time I saw him, he was alone.

In the years that followed, I returned to Sitting Bull Campground, and each time the magnificent Max was in the field having his dinner. However, the last time I was there, I scoured the area and didn't see him. Sadness was building in me, and when I was about to move on, I looked down and he was standing in the ditch right below me! He was dwarfed by the Russian thistle, Queen Anne's lace, grasses, and bushes of various types and shapes that surrounded him.

We locked eyes, and he allowed me to take his picture as he looked directly into the camera. Since I have not been back to the area, I don't know if Max still has dinner in that field by the stream, but on that night, it was truly magical seeing him. I returned to my campsite content that Max was okay.

Max on my last visit to the Bighorn Mountains

The Takeaway: Sometimes what we are looking for is right in front of us.

Story 18
The Sensual Desert

I lie in my tent awake with my eyes closed. Even behind shuttered eyelids, I am aware that the sun's light is filling my space. I hear the desert coming to life. Roosters crowing, doves cooing, wild donkeys braying, songbirds chirping, and javelinas (medium–size wild pigs) snorting as they make their morning rounds. These are the sounds I can identify.

The coyotes that had been calling through the night are now silent as they have returned to their dens. The owls and nighthawks are also quiet. I am grateful there are no buzzing insects. I feel peaceful and incredibly delicious inside; I savor the moment, letting this sensation permeate my body and soul.

It is different waking up in the city where I am not on the sun's schedule. In warm weather when my windows are open, and I am not insulated from the outdoors, I hear the traffic racing by two blocks away, the lady next door sliding her plant containers around on her patio (she does this every morning), people greeting each other, and doors slamming. On Tuesdays, I hear the garbage truck emptying the dumpsters, keeping our complex free from the trash. On Thursdays, I hear the landscapers blowing leaves or trimming bushes and trees. Everyone is busy doing their busy-ness and living their lives, and they all seem to get a much earlier start on their day than I do.

But here, I emerge from my tent with a happy heart, surrounded only by the sounds of nature. I stretch, breathing in the morning air. My tent is already warming, but the air outside remains cool. I know it will not last. In the desert, the temperature rises with the sun, and depending on the season, it can heat things quickly.

When I camped here in February, the morning was cooler and I could linger in bed until 7:30, possibly 8:00. Today I'm not aware of the time; all I know is that right now the air suits me fine.

My first task is to light the stove and heat water for coffee. I enjoy making coffee and drinking it from my old tin cup. I had a ceramic mug, but it broke. There was something decadent about sipping my morning Joe from a Santa Fe Opera mug while camping. However, after dropping it, I had to retreat to the tried-and-true tin cup my sister gave me years ago. When all is said and done, I suppose that is more appropriate, anyway.

Bird on Cactus

As I listen and watch the birds flitting around in the bushes, I wonder where they find water in this parched land. Some species tap into the huge saguaro cactus for the moisture it holds, but there must be other places to find water. Flowers, berries, and seeds probably provide some moisture. People in the area must have birdbaths the songsters could drink from, and the early morning dew on the leaves of trees and plants was another possible source. What little dew there was evaporated quickly, which explains why birds get up before the sun.

[NOTE: After Googling how desert birds get water, I learned they get liquid from the insects, as well as other prey they eat. They also have efficient kidneys so they excrete very little water. These birds were designed for desert living.]

Campers are coming to life. I can smell bacon, eggs, and pancakes cooking somewhere in the park, and it makes me hungry. It is time for breakfast. My sense of smell is always heightened when I am camping, and foods are tastier when eaten outdoors in the early morning air. Perhaps that is because I'm more in touch with my sur-roundings and, therefore, my food. At any rate, eating outdoors is a pure delight to the senses, especially in the absence of flies and mosquitoes.

The desert sunrises are not as spectacular as the sunsets. The rising sun turns the dust in the air orange as it climbs up the sky. It comes up quickly, and the color is gone just as fast, unlike the sunset which lingers. I have watched and enjoyed twilight in the desert many times.

The setting sun is an orb of golden light just before it sinks below the horizon. The dusty air around it is light-er gold. Then the sky where the orb was turns vivid gold. Gradually red, orange, pink, and violet spread out from it, while the rest of space becomes various shades of blue and gray, giving depth to the sky.

There are usually no clouds in the desert, but sometimes contrails reflect the light, leaving streaks across the sky. It's easy to think the light show is over, but I found it's wise not to turn away too quickly, as the heavens become more beautiful after the sun disappears and the afterglow appears. The hues continue to change depending on the atmospheric conditions until the heav-ens are left in darkness, and the stars begin their light show. (September 23, 2019, journal entry)

I love the desert, but I admit sometimes I am not impressed. For example, I become less conscious of my surroundings on scorching days when I am driving across the Southwest on Interstate 10. I just want to get to my destination. The heat forces me to be sealed in an air-conditioned vehicle and doesn't allow me to feel and smell the air. While I am grateful for the comfort of air conditioning, I miss that connection with my surroundings. So I amuse myself by listening to the radio or podcasts, talking on the phone (hands-free, of course), and eating Cheetos.

Not only is there little to look at, but one has to consider the possibility of haboobs, which are intense dust storms that occur regularly in dry areas. The blowing sand blots out everything and visibility is zero. There are signs along the road telling drivers what to do should they encounter one.

Two signs telling what to do in case of a Haboob

It is different when I am driving through the desert when the temperature is pleasant. I enjoy the drive and am aware of the scenery. It is no longer just sand, dust devils, haboobs, and an endless road. It is strange how my perspective changes.

What I see on a hot day in the desert

What I see on a cool day in the desert

I have found that when I allow my senses free rein, the sights and sounds allow me to feel gratitude and contentment no matter where I am. It is then that I experience the magic of the desert. An old yogic principle comes to mind.

We are either "now-here," in the present, or we are "no-where." Yogic Principle

The Takeaway: When we allow our senses to do their job, they reward us no matter where we are.

Story 19
The Prankster

As I comfortably sat at the picnic table in the RV park, I thought about being in nature and the wonderful camping trips I had experienced. Then I remembered that had not always been the case.

Some of my early camping excursions were not my choice and were miserable. When I was a teenager, camping was a family vacation and there was no question that all the family would attend. As a small child, my tent was always a safe place, but sleeping in a tent on these trips left me feeling less than safe and uncomfortable enough that I preferred staying home.

My mind drifted back to the summer of 1965. It would be the last camp outing that I did with the family of my youth.

It was a gorgeous day in the Black Hills of South Dakota. The sun was shining and a few powderpuff clouds floated across the azure sky. It seemed like it would be the perfect weather for camping. I was not sure I wanted to do this outing, but I was in the area, and my family strongly encouraged me to join them. So here I was.

I steered my Mercury Comet north on Highway 385, looking for the entrance to Roubaix Lake where I was to meet them. My husband was still in Viet Nam, so I was alone. The entrance to the park wasn't marked, but our mother said she would station my brother by the road, and he would guide me to the campsite. When I got to the area, there were no signs, and he was nowhere to be seen.

I drove up and then back down the road, looking for the turnoff, which I knew had to be close. As I approached what looked like a gravel driveway on my round trip, a kid popped out of the weeds in the ditch and ran towards my car. I slammed on the brakes. It didn't take long to realize it was my brother, but in that instant before recognition, panic seized me that a child was running into the road.

When my brother got in the car, he explained he was too embarrassed to stand out by the road, so he hid until he saw me. This sounded like him, but I was sure he had been sitting in the ditch scheming how he would torment me throughout the weekend and thought it would be funny to start by letting me look for him. He frequently played pranks on me.

Jerry wasn't always my brother.

My mother died when I was five. My dad remarried when I was eight. His new wife didn't seem to like Dad and only tolerated my three siblings and me because we were part of the package. She was pregnant and needed a father for her child, and Dad was it. She was hateful and abusive. When I was thirteen, we lived five miles out of town, but my sister managed to escape to our grandmother's house after our stepmother severely beat her.

Nana called Child Services, and when they saw my sister's battered body, they came to our house and asked the remaining three of us if we wanted to leave. I said yes and spent that summer in the children's home until Child Services could find a suitable foster family. My younger brother and sister did not leave then, but a year later they ran away.

It was after my summer at the children's home that Jerry became my brother. He was six and the oldest child in the foster family I went to live with. I never knew how or why he came up with the things he did, but I was sure he hated me and his goal was to make my life miserable. Whether or not that was his intention, he succeeded! I was now nineteen and pregnant and little had changed.

The Pup Tent

We drove to the campsite, and after greeting everyone, our mother told him to help me pitch the old, musty-smelling, canvas pup tent I was to share with our little sister. He had the tent up in short order.

As we carried the sleeping bags into the tent, he warned me not to touch the fabric if it rained, as the tent would leak. I stored that information away for future reference, not sure if it was another of his jokes. He was an Eagle Scout, so he knew about these things, but was it true? I wasn't sure.

The campsite fronted the lake, and after lunch, the younger children ran to the water for a swim. My camp duties were helping with food preparation and cleaning up after meals. With seven people, that seemed like a never-ending job. Paper plates were extravagant, so we used plastic camp ware, which made for a lot of dishes and pans to wash in the water bucket. They also had to be dried and stowed in their proper place.

I did the dishes and then donned the maternity swimsuit I had borrowed from a friend. It was red and white and had a pinafore top that went over shorts. It was heavier material than a regular swimsuit, but I liked it.

I selected an inflated inner tube and carried it to the lake for what I hoped would be a peaceful float, but with Jerry around, there was rarely a peaceful anything. Unfortunately for me, he and our sister caught a frog, and they knew exactly how to have fun with it.

Yikes! A Frog!

The two of them swam out to where I was sitting in the tube, quietly paddling around, and threw it in my lap. I did not disappoint them when I screamed and thrashed until I fell into the water. They laughed uncontrollably. Our mother scolded them, but they didn't care; my reaction was worth it.

That night it rained. Just in case Jerry was telling the truth, I lay still, making sure nothing touched the tent wall; I did not want it leaking and adding to the cold clamminess I was already experiencing. The ground was damp and the tent floor absorbed the moisture. Now the air was wet too. After the rain stopped, I finally slept for a couple of hours, but it was not a restful sleep.

The next day, I wanted to go home, but as I said, this was a family outing and there was no question but that I remain there. Before I knew it, the sun was gone and it was dark again.

That night, I awoke to find Jerry leaning over me in my tent. Being awakened that way scared the bejeebers out of me. That was no doubt part of his plan, as well as to tell me that our brother Dana had to be taken to the emergency room because he had an asthma attack. A disgruntled part of me thought it was little wonder in this cold, damp air. When our parents returned, they said the doctor had given Dana medication, and he was now breathing normally.

Camping in those days was not fun for me. It was an experience I could easily have done without. Being cold and clammy, and sleeping on the hard ground made it very unpleasant; being pregnant also didn't help. For me, it was enough to enjoy nature with a picnic. I saw no need to spend a restless night in a damp sleeping bag, wondering if I would get wet or be carried off by a serial killer. Why would I sleep like that when I had a perfectly good bed at home?

Over the years, that attitude changed, as I learned ways to stay warm and dry in a tent. Camping became an activity I enjoy, and I also understand why people invest in trailers and motorhomes.

Recently, I returned to Roubaix Lake campground where there is now a national forest sign marking the entrance. The campsites have all been updated and numbered. And I didn't see any serial killers!

Roubaix Lake Campground Sign

Jerry and I are now grown. We rarely see each other but we made peace long ago.

The Takeaway: If it rains, don't touch the tent!

Story 20
River Run

After ruminating on my early dislike for camping, I asked myself when I began enjoying it. It was the spring of 1974, and I was looking through the day's junk mail.

Included was a brochure for a weekend boating trip that starts in the town of Green River, Utah, travels down the Green River, and then up the Colorado River to Moab, Utah. This annual Memorial Day Weekend event takes the same route in southeastern Utah that explorer Major John Wesley Powell took in the late 1800s. The *Friendship Cruise,* as it is called, began in 1958 and has taken place every year since then, unless water levels were too low.

The cruise begins on Friday. The trip is 184 miles and the boats start pulling off the river late Sunday afternoon, but some do not complete the trip until Monday. This sponsored event is officially over and everyone is to be off the river by noon on Monday if they want their rig transported from Green River. The time to complete the trip is different for each boat because some people spend more time than others exploring the many natural and historic sites along the way. I suspect the amount of partying they do also influences their timing.

The year we went, the fee for this well-organized cruise included transportation of our vehicle from Green River to Moab, a chili cook-off after the cruise, rescue boats, launching and docking facilities, and radio communications for emergency messages. Since no one had cell phones in the 1970s, radio communication was important. Gas pumps and emergency services were stationed along the route, as well as a few concession items, but otherwise, the boaters took everything they needed with them.

This trip would require sleeping in a tent, but it seemed worth it to make the river run. Over the years, I had learned more about camping and what is required to make it enjoyable. I love the outdoors and being able to sleep out is fun if my body is comfortable.

I learned that sleeping *under* the bag, instead of *in* it, was warmer because I didn't suck in cold air every time I turned over. A lightweight blanket between the bag and me also helped with that and a mat between me and the ground did wonders for staying warm and off the rocks. A tent with a plastic floor was the best way to keep ground moisture from getting inside. These adjustments allowed camping to take on a whole new life for me.

It would be an ideal vacation for our family. We enjoyed taking our 15-foot, open-hull Glastron to lakes where the older girls water skied, but we had never taken the boat down a river. When we lived in Alabama, we spent weekends on the Tennessee River, but that is more like a lake than a river, so in my book, that didn't count. This was going to be a new adventure for us. The organizers created a program that allowed it to be a fun, safe event for everyone.

15' Open-Hull Glastron

Just before the trip, I injured my back, but despite the discomfort I was experiencing, I still planned to participate in this unusual weekend. We had made the reservations and most of the packing was done. I could comfortably stand and lie down, but I doubted I could sit in a bouncing boat without pain. I could stand by the sun canopy, and with all the camping gear, we could make a bed if I had to lie down. Everything would be fine.

The day finally arrived, and our family of five and the dog piled into the Mercury station wagon that my husband called his *rolling living room*. Even by 1970 standards, it was a big car, and it did feel like we took part of the house with us when we traveled. With the boat hitched behind, we headed west from our home in Golden, Colorado, on Interstate 70 to begin our adventure.

We arrived in Green River and checked in with a staff member who provided an information sheet and directions to the docks. We followed the protocol for getting the boat launched, which meant sitting in line with the boat ready to be quickly offloaded.

Once we dropped the boat, we tied up at the dock. The kids and I were to wait there while my husband went to park the rig. He wanted me in the boat in case it broke loose in the river's strong current. I wasn't sure what I would do if it did, but I guess he felt better that someone was in it. He probably never considered the possibility that the kids and I would make the trip without him if the powerful river current carried us away.

The energy at the dock was frenetic, and it was unnerving waiting for him to return, as there were about 600 boats of all sizes and descriptions on the river or nearby waiting for their turn to launch. People were shouting at each other above the noise of the river. Boat motors were churning up the water. Launch vehicles were throwing gravel as they tried to get up the boat ramp. I was glad when my husband finally got back. We untied the ropes and immediately we were swept down the river. Ready or not, we were underway!

Once we were floating, the water flow didn't seem as fast as it had sitting there waiting to be unleashed. It was like riding Japan's bullet train, which travels 199 mph as it whizzes by the landscape, yet when you are on board, it feels no faster than riding in a car.

We spent part of that first day acclimating to the water currents and our new surroundings. As we became accustomed to the river and felt at ease, we enjoyed the beautiful scenery of flowing water, small rapids, red rock formations, old ruins, and especially the Indian paintings high on the canyon walls. We wondered how the people got that high to paint. We saw dark spots on the cliffs and imagined they were ancient caves.

Green River, UT

We could camp anywhere along the river, which, despite all the boats, worked well because there were plenty of places and not everyone traveled the same distance in a day. In the late afternoon, we began looking for the perfect spot to set up camp.

We found a flat area where the water was shallow and calm, so we did not have to worry about the boat being battered on the rocks or floating downstream during the night. There was room to have dinner, pitch the tent, and explore. I remembered this place as quite lovely, but when I asked my daughter what she remembered about the trip, she said all the *cow pies* (cow manure) where we camped! She reminded me that this spot was not as ideal as my memory had recorded it.

Green River, UT

The kids helped their dad haul the camping equipment from the boat and get the tent set up, while the dog ran around marking his territory, and I cooked dinner. I made Frito pie in a cup which was sloppy joe mix over corn chips served in a cup. The kids loved it.

I don't remember where the idea came from, but it was probably a dish my Camp Fire Girls made. The organization had many easy recipes that no matter how fussy kids were, they would enjoy eating what was prepared. On our trips, the girls did the cooking, and we carried limited supplies, so meals needed to be easy and something they would eat.

After dinner and cleanup, the girls played in the shallow water and looked for pretty rocks. We explored the area until the sun disappeared behind the cliffs.

The next day, we were up early, ready to continue our adventure. I cooked breakfast and prepared sandwiches for lunch while the family repacked the boat. We ate and then resumed our float down the river.

As I suspected, I stood most of the day and held onto the shade canopy when we came to rough water. I had an unobstructed view of the cliffs and canyon ahead and knew I would have been standing anyway, even if I could have sat. We pulled off the river a few times to stretch, have lunch, and explore. Later in the day, we chose a spot to spend the night. We found a flat place and motored our way to the beach. There were no cow pies at this site.

Boat Docked & Kids Playing

The kids scouted the area. The dog was glad to be off the boat. I don't think he thought the adventure was as cool as his humans. After a campfire, s'mores, and lots of talk about our day, we retired to the tent. We had to gingerly step over the mishmash of beds, clothing, and tote bags to reach our designated sleeping bags. As I looked around inside the tent, I wondered how all these things fit in our small boat. Once we were settled, we quickly drifted into sleep.

The next morning, we were up with the sun. This was the day we had been waiting for; we would go through the confluence of the Green and Colorado Rivers. It was the primary reason people made the trip and

146

the thrill we had geared up for. After the ritual of eating breakfast and repacking the boat, we were back on the water.

We were not sure what to expect when we got to where the rivers merged, but the staff had said it would be a bumpy ride. Long before we reached the confluence, we could hear the rushing river. As we got closer, the current increased, and the water churned and boiled up as it crashed over the half-hidden boulders. With life jackets on and tense with excitement, we were quickly caught in the swift-moving current. It was exciting and scary at the same time. There was no turning back!

We bounced our way through the raging rapids, and after some tense minutes, things smoothed out and we were going up the Colorado River. We did it!

It was exhilarating for the girls and me, but not the buzz my husband wanted. He didn't think it was that exciting, so once we got free of the rapids, he turned the boat around and took us back through them to see if he could get a bigger adrenalin rush. When he tired of it, we continued on our way.

After surviving the big event, we were hungry and stopped to move around off the boat and have lunch. We still had about 50 miles to reach Moab. We pulled off the water once more and then cruised up the river without incident.

The staff was waiting for us when we arrived in Moab. They called for our rig, and it arrived as we finished our chili dinner. We loaded the boat onto the trailer and started the 350-mile drive home.

We were tired from the fresh air and the experiences of the last few days. The girls and the dog curled up and slept. There was no squabbling; it was a quiet ride home.

Over the years, we took many vacations, but this was my favorite camping trip with the family. The beautiful scenery we had cruised through could only be seen from the water, and we never knew what to expect around each bend. My back pain was minimal. The weather was perfect. There were no mosquitoes. There were no feuds between the girls, and the dog was a real trooper. The river was a challenge, but not so much that I felt overwhelmed. It was a perfect family vacation. It had been all I had hoped it would be.

The Takeaway: Create family memories. They are a blessing to all, despite the cow pies you may encounter.

Story 21
Let the Dance Begin

International Peace Day is a United Nations-sanctioned holiday. It is celebrated around the world on September 21st. Through no great planning on my part, I was in Ajo, Arizona, for the 2019 celebration of this annual event. I had no intention of attending the festivities; my only purpose for being in town was that I wanted to follow through on my idea of having a winter home there and traveling in the summer.

I arrived on September 15th and spent the week researching and looking at homes for sale. Things had not been going well in my search, and I was hot and tired but decided I needed a distraction, so I went to the Plaza to check out the festivities. I was not disappointed.

At the beginning of all events, the town's three primary cultures, Mexican, Native, and Anglo, are honored. They then read the ten ideals, which are peace, respect, hope, caring, love, happiness, dignity, environment, sharing, and friendship. From what I had experienced that last week, I was not sure these principles always carried over into everyday life, but it certainly was a worthy goal and did exist during the fiestas.

The Peace Day activities began at 5:00 p.m. and continued through the evening. The high school band and costumed performers marched in a parade from the school campus to the Plaza, which is a matter of a few blocks. (Remember, this is a tiny town.) When they arrived, they were greeted by lively DJ music and delicious-smelling food prepared by vendors.

Since I had to convince myself to go, I arrived after the parade, but in time to watch and take photos of the dance performances. As the sun sank lower in the sky, the temperature cooled to about 80 degrees, a welcome relief after the 98 degrees during the day. It was quite pleasant, and I was glad that I made the effort to join the celebration.

Young Male Dancer

Amongst the dancers, there were a few young boys and women, but most of the performers were girls aged four through teens. The three dance groups appeared to be divided by age and experience. Each had its routine and a costume that enhanced that dance.

There were many young girls in the Polynesian dance group. They had elaborate headpieces made of flowers, greens, and tall spikes. They wore pink off-one-shoulder crop tops and white grass skirts with green tassels at the hips that bounced as they danced. Some had long white tassels that hung from their wrists and a flower necklace that matched the headdress. Most of them knew the moves and performed with big smiles, especially when family members called out to them. Some closely watched the leader and followed her. A few of the smaller ones looked as if they were shell-shocked; they went through the movements probably from body memory and seemed far removed from what they were doing.

Young Island Dancers

Hula Dancers

The next group had only seven girls, and they danced the hula. They wore the same pink top as the younger girls, but their skirts were made of flowered cloth that was gathered at the waist. They all had long black hair and sported a pink hibiscus over one ear. These girls knew the steps and were fluid in their movements. I thought of my niece, who used to dance the hula and often chided, "Watch the hands."

Some of the older girls and adult women performed traditional dances. They wore multi-colored ribbons in their hair and costumes made of bright fabrics; orange, pink, blue, yellow, and green. Their dresses were decorated with multi-colored striping around the neck, waist, and bottom of the skirt. Their vibrant attire floated and swirled as they performed.

A Traditional Dancer

The dancers were excited to be performing and paid no attention to traffic noise from the nearby street or the kids chasing each other around the area designated as the stage. High school girls that were not part of the dance teams did their line dances in the grass between the performances. The adults sat on the green and ate picnics they had brought with them or food they had purchased from the vendors.

When the dance groups finished their performances, the high school band gathered their instruments and lined up to present a concert. I listened for a while, but it had been a long day and I was exhausted, so I walked back to the car and drove the three blocks to the campground. Yes, I drove! Like I said, I was tired!

Ajo's festivities were a beautiful way to celebrate peace and honor all cultures from the desert to the islands. Food, dance, and music created a magical combination that brought people together in joy and celebration.

Watching these children giving their all, while dressed in rainbow-colored costumes, was a perfect way to observe International Peace Day. For me, it was also a great way to take my mind off of the challenges I had been having and create peace within me.

The Takeaway: Sometimes a joyful distraction is just what we need in the middle of a stressful time.

Story 22
The Ranger's Advice

In my early days of camping in the national for-ests, there was no option to reserve a camping site online; whoever arrived first got the spot. It was during that time that five friends and I went camping in the Bighorn Mountains.

We drove through many of the campgrounds, but it was a holiday weekend and there were few sites left to choose from. The only place we found that would ac-commodate all of our tents was near a swampy area. Despite the soggy ground we'd have to circumvent to get to each other's space, there were dry places to pitch our tents and gather for dinner, so we naively took it. The one thing we didn't realize was that mosquitoes breed in mountainous wet areas and feed on humans just as they do at lower elevations.

Since this turned into a less-than-ideal experience, I asked a ranger when the best time to tent camp in the Bighorn Mountains was. He told me September, and I believed him; why wouldn't I? So the next time I packed up my gear for a few days away from the city, I went in September.

It was drizzling rain and chilly when I arrived at Sitting Bull Campground. There were few campers, and those that were there were in RVs with generators run-ning. I began setting up my tent. As I was working, a lady in the rig close by asked if I wanted some soup they had just made. I thanked her and declined.

At that time in my life, I was unable to accept help, as it seemed to imply that I was not doing things well enough and was incapable of taking care of myself. I was always willing to help others but could not accept it for myself. Since that time, I have learned to graciously accept gifts and help from others. But I was different back then.

After I pitched my tent, I ate my Progresso soup, and as I recall, I ate it cold out of the can. My hands were cramped with the chill, and I wondered how long I could stay in this weather. I walked to the restroom, and another camper asked if I would like some firewood. It seemed *The Girl in the Tent* needed some looking after! I thanked him and again turned down the offer. It was a pleasant idea to have a fire, but I couldn't accept his wood, and besides, it was too cold to sit out even with a fire. I just wanted to snuggle into my bed.

Before I went into the tent, I heated water and filled my thermos, so I could have tea in bed the next morning. I packed everything but the tent and its contents into the car. There were two reasons for this. I didn't want it to get wet, and I also didn't want animals rummaging through it. Besides warming a thermos of water, this proved to be the smartest thing I did on that trip!

Once tucked into bed, I slept well until 3:00 in the morning when I awoke. Despite being buried in blankets and having my coat over my head, my body was freezing. Something had to be done. I was already dressed, as it was too cold the night before to get undressed. I got up, started the car, turned the heater up to high, and began dragging everything out of the tent. It was dark, and I didn't notice right away, but as I started taking the tent down, ice slid off of it. There was a half-inch of ice covering the tent! How cold was it anyway? No wonder I was freezing!

I shook off the remaining ice, stuffed the wet tent into a large black trash bag, and pushed it into the backseat of the car, along with everything else I had hurriedly packed. Since nothing was neatly folded, it took some effort to jam it all into the car. When I got to civilization, the tent would have to be set up in the sun so it could completely dry out, or I would have an issue with mildew.

Very Cold!

When I finished loading the vehicle, I dropped into the driver's seat. The heater was doing its job, and the car was starting to get warm. I sat there rubbing my hands, trying to thaw out. I was grateful I had packed everything outside the tent the night before. Then I re-

156

membered the thermos of water I had heated. It was no longer hot, but it was warm enough to make tea. I wrapped my hands around the cup and sipped for a few minutes, while I pondered what to do next. The hot springs in Thermopolis came to mind. Yes, that was exactly what I needed!

Thermopolis, Wyoming, is a town of 3000 people and has several hot spring pools of different temperatures that I knew would quickly take the chill from me; they were wonderful to soak in. It was a two-hour drive, so I would get there about the time the town was waking up. I could get a hot breakfast and then do a soak. In the meantime, the car heater was working and I would soon be at a lower elevation where it was bound to be warmer. I had a plan and quietly slipped out of the campground.

I stopped in Ten Sleep on the way to Thermopolis, thinking I might get breakfast there, but nothing was open. As I walked down the main street, I read a wooden sign that said the Native Indians named Ten Sleep. The name came from the fact that it took ten days (ten sleeps) on foot to get to that area from Fort Laramie, Yellowstone, or Casper, depending on what direction you were coming from. I appreciated how the Natives were so descriptive in naming things, even if you had to know the story before it made sense.

When I arrived in Thermopolis at 6:00 a.m., a restaurant was open and breakfast was being served. I had the typical Wyoming breakfast of two eggs, hash browns, toast, and coffee. I sat longer than usual because there was plenty of time before the pools opened at 9:00. Eventually, I left the café and went to my car to take a nap. My basic needs were met. I was warm, my tummy was full, and now I could get the sleep I failed to have at the campground.

I'm not sure why the ranger said September was the best month to camp in the Bighorn Mountains. Perhaps he was basing his information on people staying in RVs, there being no mosquitoes, or that there were fewer tourists then. There is one reason for all of these being true; September nights in the mountains are freezing! From my experience, July and August are the best times to tent camp in the Bighorns. It gets chilly at night, but I have never had ice on the tent; I have always been able to stay warm, even the night my tent flooded.

The Takeaway: In September, it is still hot in the desert, and it is freezing in the mountains. Choose wisely.

Story 23
Bear Lodge

Throughout the world, there are many Peace Day celebrations, such as the one I attended in Ajo. It is good that we pause and recognize our connection with all life.

The Native Americans have established another annual event that focuses on peace. This day is celebrated in June and is known as World Peace and Prayer Day. I was fortunate to experience the beginning of this annual event, but at the time, I did not know the significance.

Bear Lodge/Devil's Tower, Wyoming

All I knew was this was a *gathering of tribes* and that all people were welcome to attend. This was unusual because Wasichu (White People) often were not welcome at Native American events. Although I did not know the purpose of the gathering, I was there because someone had told me about it and I felt drawn to attend. So I packed up my tent, ice chest, and a few other necessities and drove two hours to *Mato Tipila* (Native American for *Bear Lodge*) or, as it is commonly called, *Devil's Tower*.

I could see the Tower long before I reached it, as its imposing presence rises 867 feet above the surrounding land and measures 1000 feet in diameter. The American Indian tribes have different legends about how this geologic anomaly formed. But no matter what legend they ascribe to it, they all hold it as sacred land. It was primarily the 1977 movie *Close Encounters* that caused it to achieve prominence with other folks around the world.

The National Park Service manages the park and there are about twenty tribes that presently have a cultural affiliation with this area, including the Lakota, Cheyenne, Arapaho, Crow, and Kiowa. Throughout June, many Natives come to Bear Lodge to perform indigenous religious practices. The most auspicious date is June 21st, which is the summer solstice. They feel solstice is a powerful time to pray for peace and harmony among all beings. The gathering I was attending was the weekend of June 21, 1996.

On this date, World Peace and Prayer Day (WPPD), not to be confused with the Day of World Peace (which is in September), convened for the first time. WPPD was born from a vision Chief Arvol Looking Horse, the Nineteenth Generation Keeper of the Sacred White Buffalo Calf Woman Pipe, had when the first white buffalo calf was born in 1994. The prophecy said:

When earth and climate changes begin to disrupt the natural cycle of survival and life, the animals will warn with their sacred color white. This will be a sign of what is called the Crossroads; either to be faced with chaos, disasters, and witness tears from our relative's eyes, or we can unite spiritually in this Global Community—All Nations, All Faiths, One Prayer.

To understand the significance of the White Buffalo Calf Woman Pipe and what it means to be the keeper of it, we need to look at its story, which took place nineteen generations ago during a time of famine. The tribal chief sent two young men out to hunt for food. As they traveled, they saw a white cloud in the distance, and from it, they saw a beautiful woman with dark hair wearing white buckskin.

One man told the other that he wanted her for his wife, but the other could see she was holy and warned him it would be dangerous to do anything disrespectful. The man approached her anyway, and a cloud enveloped them, and when it disappeared, only the woman and a pile of bones remained. The guy watching was frightened, but she told him to come forward, as she could see his heart was pure and that he did not want to possess her. He moved slowly towards her.

161

The woman explained that she had supernatural powers. She said that he was to return to his camp and call the council to prepare a feast for her arrival. The Creator had sent this sacred woman to teach the people how to pray to ensure a future of harmony, peace, and balance. She became a primary prophet of the Lakota.

To perform this prayer, she brought the Lakota Nation a sacred ceremonial pipe, which is called the White Buffalo Calf Woman Pipe. Smoking this pipe is not like smoking cigarettes with a friend; it is a sacred ceremony and is considered a holy and powerful prayer.

The other significant part of this story concerns the white buffalo calf. These bison are not albinos. They are white at the time of birth and turn brown as they age. They are extremely rare. It is estimated that there was only one born out of every one million births, and since 1994, according to some records, there have been dozens.

The white calf was the last of the four colors: brown, yellow, and red calves to be born. A white buffalo calf with black hooves, nose, and eyes was born in 1994. Her name was *Miracle,* and the Lakota considered her the most sacred living thing on earth. Her birth signaled the time for global healing and for mending the sacred hoop. Miracle was a symbol of hope.

A White Buffalo Calf

Chief Arvol Looking Horse knew this triggered the beginning of the changes. He never thought he would see this happen in his lifetime, but he knew the prophecies well. The birth of a white buffalo calf is a sign that prayers are being heard and that the promises of the prophecy are being fulfilled. And it is a warning that there is a need for hearts and heads to come together to heal the earth. For this to happen, world leaders have to connect in a circle where none is more important than another.

This 1996 event set in motion the mending of the sacred hoop. To honor the sacredness of this gathering, many people rode on horseback from Wahpeton, Saskatchewan, Canada to Bear Lodge (Devil's Tower) in the Black Hills of Wyoming. This was a spiritual journey known as the *Unity Ride*.

Riders had not come together for this sacred ride for over 100 years, so they began preparing by doing a journey each year, beginning in 1993. Their goal was to unite the tribes as they rode the 450 miles to their destination. It is worth mentioning here that one of their stops on the way to Devil's Tower was at the Bighorn Medicine Wheel, mentioned in another Story.

The riders had arrived before me, and their horses were grazing in the corral. As I drove through the campground, I saw the sites were all occupied and many people already had their camps set up. I stopped and talked to a man about what my options might be, and he invited me to share their site.

The Park Service had rules about how many people could occupy a site, but this family had room for another tent. I expressed gratitude, as it was the best site ever! It was close to the chief's circle where they chanted and drummed until the early morning hours AND I had a view of the Tower. It was perfect.

I arranged my tent so it was facing Bear Lodge. By the time I went to bed, the drumming had begun. I lay on my mat, staring out the tent screen at the outline of the formation, which I could barely make out in the dark. There wasn't much moonlight and clouds were gathering.

I listened as the large, circular drums thundered well into the night. It was comforting to feel their pulsing beat as I slid in and out of consciousness. I could feel the importance of the chanting that accompanied the rhythmic sound. Sometime during the night, the drumming stopped, and a soft rain fell. It seemed fortuitous as it cleaned the air and prepared the energies for the weekend ahead.

It had been my experience that attending a Native American event means there is no concrete timetable for when things begin. There may be a loose schedule, but everyone just seems to know when it is time to head to the sweat lodge, the dinner area, or the assembly. So it surprised me there was a gathering scheduled in the field for 10:00 a.m. Not that it would begin at 10:00, but that was the plan.

Before the assigned time, people picked up the items they wanted with them and walked to the designated area. The Native American events I had attended in the past were much looser in enforcing the rules. Here, protocols had to be closely followed if one wanted to join the gathering, and I was not familiar with most of them.

The one that almost kept me from entering the circle was that women were required to wear a skirt. It never occurred to me to bring such clothing on a camping trip, plus I'm not even sure I owned a skirt. The guard told me I couldn't enter without one, and I felt disappointed that I could not attend. Then it occurred to me I was carrying a poncho that I intended to use as my sit-upon. I put the poncho around my waist. It was practically falling off, but it fulfilled the requirement, and the man in charge allowed me to enter.

I found a spot in the circle and sat down. Some weeds were poking me, and it was not as comfortable as if I had folded my poncho under me, but it worked. I sat and stared at people and their colorful clothing. No one seemed upset that the program did not begin as scheduled; they walked around and visited with friends. Bear Lodge was visible beyond the knoll, and I enjoyed just sitting and listening to the conversations as I gazed at my surroundings.

Finally, the announcer took the microphone and laid the ground rules for what they expected of the participants. He announced another protocol I didn't know about and that was women on their moon cycle had to move to the outer field. He said that a man on horseback would ride around and he could tell if they were, so they may as well go now. No one else seemed to be surprised by this announcement; I guess it was just this naïve Wasichu.

There were prayers and presentations, and the theme was the restoration of peace and balance. The highlight was when Chief Arvol Looking Horse presented the White Buffalo Calf Woman Pipe. I don't know if there was a White Buffalo Calf Woman, or if any of the legends about her are true, but I do know the energy of peace filled the air when they held up the pipe. As I recall, they did not remove the pipe from the animal skins it was wrapped in, but just its presence brought a feeling of reverence and harmony. It may seem strange that a pipe could do this.

Perhaps the energy of White Buffalo Calf Woman was imbued in the pipe, or the prayers and beliefs of people who smoked it over the 19 generations had affected it. This group of people coming together and focusing on peace also generated that feeling. While some may debate the source of this peace, all I can say is that it felt nice. I may not have understood the Native traditions, but it was a special moment, and I felt blessed to be there.

My camping trip to Devil's Tower turned into a spiritual journey that I had not expected. It just felt important that I attend the gathering, despite not knowing it was the beginning of an event that would become an annual global occurrence.

1996 was the first World Peace and Prayer Day, but it didn't stop there. Each year, Chief Arvol Looking Horse travels to one of the four directions of the world presenting the message of world peace.

Know that you yourself are essential to this world. Understand both the blessing and the burden of that. You yourself are desperately needed to save the soul of this world. Did you think you were put here for something less? In a Sacred Hoop of Life, there is no beginning and no end.

We ask all people of all faiths to respond and support our efforts towards world peace and harmony—our circle of life where there is no ending and no beginning. We ask the global community to pray with us, whether it is in nature, a church, temple, synagogue, mosque, or wherever the spirit may guide you to pray with us on this day.

Chief Arvol Looking Horse
19th Generation Keeper of the
White Buffalo Calf Woman Pipe

Google World Peace and Prayer Day to see where and how you can participate.

Story 24
A Mouse in My Tent

WARNING: If you are a rodent lover or squeamish, you may want to skip this Story.

To understand this account, I have to take you back to when I was nine years old. My dad built a house in the country, and when we moved in, so did the mice. They infested our home. Every night, I lay in bed and listened as they ran through the house squeaking as only mice can do. I don't know if there were exterminators back then, but even if there were, Dad would not have called one. Instead, he bought bags of traps, and before bed, my sister and I were charged with loading them with cheese and placing them around the house. Since the kitchen was their primary gathering spot, we focused our efforts on that area.

The traps were not like the failsafe plastic ones today. They had a flat wooden base, to which wire fastenings were attached. There was a place to bait the trap, and when the mouse tried to take the bait, the spring would snap, usually catching the mouse. It was a very delicate operation loading the traps, and it had to be done just right, or they would spring prematurely, catching little fingers in the mechanism.

My sister and I had a bedroom that was close to the kitchen, and I could hear their claws clicking on the linoleum floor as they ran from cupboard to cupboard.

It was a horrible sound that was topped only by the noise of a springing trap. When a mouse touched one, the wire sprang on them. It wasn't always instant death, and the wooden wedge would slap the floor as the overabundant and obnoxious pests tried to free themselves. It was an awful sound and a horrifying experience for this child.

Old Style Mouse Trap

If we went into the kitchen and turned on the light, we could watch them scatter under the cabinets, stove, and refrigerator. It was disgusting to open a cupboard drawer and see their droppings, or worse yet, have one jump out. We packed our school lunches in the evening and they were fair game if we didn't keep them in the refrigerator. Mice were a scourge from my childhood. Knowing this may help you understand my reaction to the horrifying event I experienced that night.

Stay with me one more minute as I give you a little more background information. There has only been one thing that has ever entered my tent uninvited, and that was a parade of ants that chewed their way through the tent floor. This was years ago in California, and it was my fault, as I had placed my tent too near their anthill.

It wasn't a big deal when I found the hole they made, because it happened during the day and they were gone when I came back in the evening, so they didn't bite or crawl on me while I slept. While it didn't bother me, it may have upset the ants, since the tent interfered with their march to and from their nest. My response was simple; I moved my tent. Since then, I have made sure I am nowhere near an ant mound when I pitch my tent. With this precaution having been taken, I was not expecting any visitors. Now that you have the backstory, let's move on to my experience.

It was a warm night. The fan hummed me to sleep. I was lying on my stomach with my feet dangling over the end of my air mattress. I had a sheet over me, but my feet were exposed. I felt safe here in the RV park because I had no reason not to.

I was startled out of a sound sleep by something touching my foot. It didn't take long to realize it was a mouse, and it was chewing on my big toe! Startled, I did what any paranoid person would do.

I flipped on the light and sat up screaming, as I watched it run around the tent frantically trying to escape. There was no one to help or save me; this was up to me. I looked for something to hit it, and the hammer was the only thing handy. I grabbed it and started swinging. (Later, upon reflection, I saw the flaw in this.) I struck again and again, but it maneuvered quickly and agilely. It disappeared. There was no way I was going back to sleep with that *thing* in my tent.

It was dark outside, but I got up and began hauling everything out of the tent, shaking it as I did. I took one article at a time, waving it again and again through the air. Once everything was on the picnic table, I again shook each piece separately before returning it to the tent. I was very thorough in checking all my things, but I never found the mouse. This did not comfort me, as I would have preferred to see it scurry off into the night.

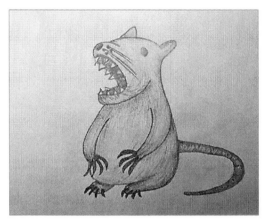

The Toe-Biting Mouse

Did I shake it off of whatever it was clinging to? Did it run out as the crazy woman scrambled in and out of the tent? I don't know where it went, but when I finished, it was not in the tent and that was all I cared about. I knew that because I was thorough, and once everything was back in the tent, I did not see it or hear its little feet scratching the plastic tent floor.

I searched to find how the mouse got into the tent, as I never wanted that to happen again. I found I did not get the side and bottom zippers tightly closed where they came together, and it left a tiny opening. As everyone knows, mice can squeeze through the tiniest spaces. And this one did! I will certainly be more careful in the future.

The Takeaway: If you don't want to lose your toes, make sure your tent has no openings, even tiny ones.

Story 25
Ants and the Mountain Lion

Having the mouse in my tent took me back to when I was visiting a family in Groveland, California, a small town in the Sierra Nevada Mountains close to Yosemite National Park. Their house was a small modified A-frame, and instead of taking one of the children's beds, I slept in my tent. It was big enough for my double-sized foam mat and tote bag. It was quite comfortable and provided me with my own space.

The Home in Groveland

This was a residential area, but homes were on three-acre lots that were left natural and gave one the impression of being in the wild. I was to find out just how *wild* it was. One of the first rules of camping is to never bring food into your tent, as wild animals often look for handouts. I never keep food in my tent, but I had not thought about *myself* being the meal!

173

On the first day, despite having nothing they would want, ants chewed a hole in the tent's floor. I didn't know what they were looking for but decided it was probably just what ants do. Later, I found I had put my tent too close to the path they followed to forage for food, and they were probably as disgruntled having me there as I was for the hole they made. I moved the tent, which took care of the problem; they did not return.

The next night, I awoke to the sound of the dry manzanita leaves crunching on the backside of my tent. That sound was accompanied by deep throat rumbling of what could only be a mountain lion. He was sniffing around my tent. I could hear him breathe and mark his territory. I could even smell him! There was nothing but a piece of nylon fabric between us. If he was going to hurt me, there was little I could do.

The Mountain Lion

At first, I was frightened and lay still, waiting, not daring to breathe. Then all fear left me, and I knew I would be okay. I felt a deep peace come over me; I fell asleep. The next thing I knew, the sun was up, and I was still in one piece. I asked myself if it had been a dream. No, it wasn't; I knew it was real.

When I walked into the house, the family was excitedly talking about the mountain lion the neighbors had seen during the night. I tried to share my experience, but no one seemed to hear me. It was okay because it was enough for me to know I had remained safe, despite the perceived threat.

It didn't seem logical, but the mountain lion *outside* my tent was less frightening than the little mouse *inside* my tent chewing on my toe. No doubt my childhood memories caused my reaction to the mouse. The fact that it had brazenly entered my tent and accosted me didn't help its case. I felt safe in my tent, and then I wasn't. The mountain lion stayed *outside* my tent, and for some reason, I knew it would not harm me.

I have thought about this experience many times since then. Remembering the lion and the peaceful place I entered has helped me remain calm through other events that seemed threatening and beyond my control. Amazingly, things do work out no matter how tenuous they seem in the moment.

The Takeaway: Find and enter your peaceful place, especially when you are scared.

Story 26
Battle for a Harem

Wildlife seems to have been a major part of my wilderness adventures, and this trip was no different. However, it did not have the element of danger that the mouse, ants, and mountain lion presented. I was here completely by choice to have a magical experience.

During the last two weeks of September and the first two weeks in October, male elk have the most extreme competition of their lives. This is the time of year when they establish their dominance and build their herds. Only the strongest males have harems because they must fight other males for that privilege.

I witnessed this impressive event when I lived in Boulder, Colorado, and went to Rocky Mountain National Park. It was such a moving experience that I wanted to repeat it, so I packed my camping gear into the car and drove 50 miles to the southern Black Hills in South Dakota.

I would spend a night or two in Wind Cave National Park, which is home to a herd of elk. This National Park is the site of Wind Cave, which is known for its unique boxwork formations made of thin blades of calcite that form square shapes that protrude from the walls and ceiling; hence, the name *boxwork*. The cave has hundreds of miles of tunnels that make it the eighth-largest cave in the world. Above ground, the park includes the biggest, natural, mixed-grass prairie in the United States.

Wind Cave Boxwork Formations, SD

The park has about a million visitors per year, yet because of its vast size, it never feels crowded. Today was no different, and the campground was about half full. It might fill up later, but for now, I had plenty of spaces from which to choose. I drove around the various loops, looking for my spot. I noticed there were several other tents, which surprised me, as I am usually the only tent camper. The reason for more tents became obvious when I saw there were motorcycles parked at those sites; a tent was all the sleeping comfort the bikes could accommodate.

One camper had the tent on top of his vehicle. I wasn't sure of the advantages. It seemed the space would be limited, wild animals could still reach you, and the climb in and out could be risky if you got up in the dark. I always thought it was safer to keep food stored in my car away from my tent in case animals wanted a snack, but with this setup, you would be right on top of it. It was an innovative idea, though.

I found a site on the edge of the park next to a field. My space was grassy and had a 30-foot ponderosa pine tree under which I would place my tent. Once I decided on my campsite, I walked to the registration board, filled out the required form, and paid the fee. Someone had left a pile of cut firewood nearby, asking only for a donation. I pulled $5 from my wallet, left it in the tin can, carried three logs back to my site, and placed them in the fire ring the forest service provided. I planned to be there a night or two, so if I didn't burn it that night, I would the next.

View from My Campsite

When I got back to my site, there was a mountain bluebird with the sweetest song sitting in the pine tree that sheltered my site. He stayed there for a long time serenading me.

Blue Bird that Sang for Me

After I set up camp and had dinner, I walked to the pavilion to listen to the ranger give a nature talk. In the National Parks, rangers offer programs each evening to inform visitors about the park and the wildlife that reside there.

Since it was rutting season, the ranger focused his talk on elk and their mating rituals. The man said after the talk, he would take those who wanted to go out to an area to view the elk. He couldn't guarantee that we would see or hear anything, but this was one spot where they often congregated. Since we may want to spend a while there, he gave us time to go to our sites to gather chairs, water, snacks, binoculars, and other things we wanted to take with us.

Soon cars began forming a line with the ranger's vehicle in the lead. We followed him out of the campground and through the park. He took us to a paved lot where we parked in the designated spaces. It was a warm evening, and people got out and set up folding chairs, excitedly preparing for the event. The ranger hung around for an hour to answer questions, and then he left.

We all sat there, anticipating what was to come. Some people thought they heard an elk bugle off in the distance. Elk bugling is a very distinctive sound, and once you hear it, you never forget it. I heard the sound too, but it seemed more like a coyote howling. I didn't say so, because even if it wasn't elk, it was a thrill to hear something.

As I sat expectantly waiting, I drifted back to my first time watching the elk and the excitement I felt hearing them bugle. It was something I had wanted to do for years, and finally, my friend Peggy, who was a seasoned elk watcher, offered to be my guide. I remember that day well.

We had about an hour's drive to Rocky Mountain National Park, so we planned to leave at 3:00 in the afternoon, as the elk usually begin intensely bugling at dusk and continue into the night.

As I got ready, I told myself I was not going to a fashion show, and it was all right to dress warm and comfortably, as it would be cold in the mountains. I donned long johns, sweatpants, winter boots, and my heaviest coat and scarf. When a horn sounded, I knew it was Peggy letting me know she was outside. I grabbed my purse, binoculars, and the bag of snacks I had prepared and went out to join her. As we drove, she told stories of her elk-watching adventures, which made the trip go quickly.

The mountain sky was gray and it was cold enough to see our breath, but we were warmly dressed and armed with a thermos of hot chocolate. We drove into a parking lot and found a spot where no vehicles were obstructing our view. After turning off the engine, we put the windows down. We were close to the herd, and there was no reason to leave the comfort of the car, plus bucks can be unpredictable and dangerous when they are rutting. We had no intention of disturbing them or getting trampled!

In front of us was a relatively flat, open area. The herd we were watching had packed the snow hard. With the windows down, we could easily hear the elk calling. A magnificent bull elk stood with his head high, keeping watch over his *girls*. *Gus* made bugling sounds, which started as a low-pitched growl and rose to a high-pitched scream. He was warning other males to stay away. He did not want any of his thirty-five females wandering off with another male.

Male Elk

Part of Elk Herd

There was a small male on the edge of big Gus's group that kept trying to lure one of the females away. Gus watched him and stood at attention. Several times the intruder got too close, and Gus gave him the bugle warning and lunged in his direction. The little guy ran off but soon returned; he was not giving up easily. I imagined he was in training for when he was grown and ready to have a herd of his own.

Young Bull Elk

Gus repeated the warning, but the cow thief came back again and again. At first, the female didn't seem interested, but the longer the challenge continued, the more attentive she became. Finally, Gus decided he'd had enough and let her go with the stray. They ran into the woods.

During rutting season, bull elk do not eat or sleep for days. They have to remain ever vigilant to keep their herd together by letting other elk know they are the strongest in the forest. This is instinct, and it ensures the lineage remains strong. Charles Darwin called this "survival of the fittest."

Rutting is a grueling time for males. It can be a month of fighting, chasing, and breeding that takes its toll on them. The average bull sustains 40-60 wounds and can lose up to twenty percent of his body weight. After the rut, their job is done and they become reclusive to heal and rebuild their strength.

I was startled back to Wind Cave Park as car engines turned over. We had heard nothing and people were tired; it was time to return to their campsites. I was getting sleepy, and since I did not want to spend the night in the car, I also left. I was a bit disappointed we had heard no elk, but it was nice to be out with other people sharing a moment and reliving my previous elk experience.

Knowing it would be dark when I returned to camp, I had gathered what I wanted in the tent before I left. I quickly slipped into my shelter and was soon fast asleep.

During the night, I awoke hearing elk bugling close by. There was no denying that distinctive sound.

It continued until daylight. I lay awake for a long time, smiling as I listened. I did not see the elk, but what a treat to hear their majestic call. My wish had been fulfilled, and I could go home anytime.

The Takeaway: Often, what we want comes in its own time.

Story 27
The Rider and the Storm

The mouse, ants, and mountain lion were not the only visitors I had while camping. This story includes another critter that came calling in the night, but thankfully, he did not enter my tent.

In the late 1990s, I took my three grandsons, all under the age of ten, to Badlands National Park in South Dakota to camp. The park has a program that children can take part in to earn a Jr. Ranger Badge.

After setting up camp, we picked up the form at the visitors' center and spent the rest of the day researching the answers and recording them on the sheet provided. It was great fun, and we learned about the park and the animals that live there, and it gave structure to the boys' day. It also diminished the time they had to climb on the steep, slippery formations the park is known for.

Badlands National Park Formations

The Badlands' rugged beauty and striking geologic deposit of fossils attract visitors from around the world. The 244,000-acre National Park is protected land. This mixed-grass prairie is home to bison, bighorn sheep, coyotes, prairie dogs, jackrabbits, rattlesnakes, deer, and black-footed ferrets.

The area was named the *Badlands* by the Indigenous People because it presented many challenges. When it rained, the wet clay became slick and sticky, making it difficult for their horses to move. The jagged buttes were hard to navigate. It was cold and windy during the winter, and the summers were hot and dry. The water sources were muddy and unsafe to drink. These factors made the land difficult to survive in, and evidence of early human activity points to seasonal hunting, rather than permanent habitation.

In most national parks, there is a program in the evening when one of the park rangers presents a talk and shows slides to educate and entertain the visitors. The speakers rotate and they all have different subjects, and even after participating numerous times, I have never seen the same presentation twice. I have always found the talks interesting and well-delivered. I wondered if being able to speak in front of groups was a requirement for being a park ranger.

On one occasion, they brought out several telescopes and allowed us to look at different planets and constellations. There was also a meteor shower that night that we witnessed. Another time, a ranger spoke about the wildlife that inhabits the park. On another occasion, the talk focused on the history of the area and described the archaeological Big Pig Dig they were doing and the fossils they had found.

The Pig story began thirty-four million years ago when the Badlands had hot, moist weather, but then the climate changed and drought came to the land. The waterholes in the area dried up except for one. This meant that the animals from the surrounding land had to drink from this one pond. It became more of a wallow, and some critters ventured too far into the muddy water and got stuck.

Predators found this a feeding ground, and as they fed off those that were trapped, they also got stuck. The animals stepped on each other, pushing them further under the ground where they were soon buried. As the land continued to dry out, the animals hardened and eventually became fossilized.

Two of my Grandsons in the Badlands

I didn't know what the program was for tonight, but I was sure it would keep the boys entertained. We had dinner at our campsite, and after cleaning up, we went to the amphitheater to listen to the presentation. This one was structured differently.

The sun had set and there was no moon, so it was dark, but the ranger said we were going for a walk. He gave us time to go to our vehicles or campsites to get flashlights and blankets. When we had reassembled, he led us down a dimly lit path until it ended, and we had to turn on our flashlights. We followed him up a smooth, flat gorge into the formations; it was easy walking, even in the dark.

The Gorge

He stopped in a rocky alcove and asked that we get seated. By now, our eyes had adjusted to the dark, so once we were comfortable, we turned off our lights. He lit his lantern and opened a small, well-worn book. It was the diary of a pony express rider, whose name I don't recall. He began reading by the light of the lantern.

As we sat there, I was transported back to the 1800s. The thought occurred to me that the only thing that could make this evening more authentic was a campfire, but they were only allowed in the designated fire rings. Sitting in the dark, with the only light coming from the lantern, we were all mesmerized by the stories that unfolded.

The pony express riders rode ten miles an hour for 75 miles. They were given a fresh horse every ten to fifteen miles. Pony stations were located five to fifteen miles apart depending on the terrain, which determined how far the horse could travel. Besides these stations, the pony express used stagecoach stops and sometimes ranches.

When one rider completed his part of the journey, he handed his bag to another rider. The sack of mail traveled around the clock to cover the 1,966-mile route from Missouri, through Kansas, Nebraska, Colorado, Wyoming, Utah, and Nevada, and ending in California. This took ten days, which was record timing for delivering a letter in the 1800s.

One particular story was about the young rider's encounter with an Indian. He had been warned that they shot at anything, so when he saw one on the trail, he grabbed his gun, hung off the side of his horse, and rode as fast as he could. The Indian shot but missed, and he escaped. Another thing the boy mentioned was that he felt important because the people were so excited to get their mail that they had cookies, cakes, and bread waiting for him when he arrived at the station. The excitement those people felt may be hard for us to imagine today. With phones, texting, and email, we have instant communication and seldom even use the post office.

This rider was like the others in that he was young and only weighed 100 pounds. The company preferred the riders to be small because the horses could travel faster with less weight.

Unlike many of the others, this boy was not an orphan. This may seem strange to mention, but the company favored orphans, as they did not want families complaining if their son died. According to historical records, in the eighteen months the express was in business, eight riders died on the job. Four of them died from Indian attacks, one was hanged for killing someone, one died in an unrelated accident, and two froze to death.

Horse on the Prairie

Their motto may sound familiar, as a variation of it was used by the postal system for many years. It was, "Neither rain, nor snow, nor the death of night, can keep us from our duty." The company ended after only eighteen months in service, because Western Union completed the transcontinental telegraph line in 1861, making the pony express obsolete.

After listening to the ranger read these stories, it was easy to imagine the adventures this young rider had, as he swiftly rode across the desolate prairie to a station where he dropped the bag of mail. He was then free to rest until a pouch came from the opposite direction, which he carried back the way he had come.

These stories made me appreciate the life these young men lived. I had thought it was a routine job riding as fast as they could across the open land. I never considered the prairie storms, outlaws, Indians, and wild animals they encountered. Traveling in the cold winter or the summer heat presented even more challenges. Hearing this diary read made me realize that these brave young people were frequently presented with situations that threatened their survival.

My boys listened attentively as the ranger read. They didn't even fiddle with their flashlights! The program showed them a very different life from their own, and it seemed they were envisioning themselves making the mail run.

After the ranger finished reading, we walked back to our campsite. My boys had had a busy day, and by the time we returned to the tent, they were ready for lights out. As they fell asleep, they told their own stories, mostly those containing *toilet talk*. They didn't seem to mind that the four of us were crammed into my little tent. Kids seem to sleep anywhere, especially when they are tired and feel safe.

Soon after they faded into slumberland, a storm started. I was relieved that we were all in one tent; if they did wake, at least I would be there for them. The wind blew with fury and rocked the tent while rain pounded it. My tent had taken me through storms before, and I gave thanks it was a sturdy dome that didn't bend like the straight wall tents. I peeked out and saw non-stop lightning shooting sideways across the sky, while thunder cracked. I kept checking to make sure the kids remained covered and dry. They slept!

The storm lasted two hours and the boys never stirred. It was beyond me how they could sleep through all the noise, but I was grateful they had. It would have been upsetting to all of us if these little guys were afraid and crying or, worse yet, wanting to go out to play in the rain.

My Grandsons and Me

When they woke in the morning, they had no idea what had taken place and did not believe me when I told them what they had slept through. It wasn't until they saw the damage done in the campground that they decided there really had been a storm. Awnings had blown off motorhomes and people's possessions and trash were everywhere.

It further piqued their interest when we found a snake that had crawled under our tent to stay dry. My youngest grandson was fearful at the thought that it could have come into the tent, but I assured him there was no way it could do that because the tent was tightly sealed. However, that thought had crossed my mind too. For the older boys, it was cool and validated the story of the storm.

Perhaps the boys didn't wake during the storm because they were dreaming they were pony express riders delivering mail in a storm. Was it all part of their dream?

The Takeaway: Sometimes critters just want to stay warm and dry.

Story 28
The Coyote's Song

While I was camping in Ajo, I had plenty of time for reflection on my past journeys into the wilderness. I recalled when Alexandria and her friend LuAnn came to visit me in Rapid City, South Dakota. They had not camped in the Badlands, so we took our camping gear and went to Badlands National Park for the night. Lu-Ann was not an outdoorsy person and did not hesitate to let us know that, but she came anyway.

We intended to camp at the main campground by the visitor's center because it had picnic tables, water, and restroom facilities. However, it was full, so we went to another part of the park where I had often camped.

Sage Creek Campground is a rustic area. It has no designated spaces, tables, or running water, but it does have a vault toilet and a hitching post to tie up horses. This area can accommodate horse people, as well as anyone else who chooses to stay there.

I liked staying at Sage Creek because most campers preferred the main campground, so it was less crowded and I liked that the wild buffalo wandered through the area. I usually camped alone, so for a change, it was nice to have company and introduce them to the wonders of this wilderness area.

They set up their tent, and I assembled mine close to theirs. After we had the basics taken care of, we ate the dinner we had picked up from the store on the way out of town. The sun was setting, making it a lovely time to drive through the land of jagged peaks. The dimming light cast shadows on the formations that gave depth and beauty to the barren land.

South Dakota Badlands

We stopped in the parking lot next to the prairie dog town. Some of the critters were standing up next to their burrows. They were keeping watch and would let the rest of their village know if danger was nearby. They were chattering in "prairiedogese" to warn them that we were there. This group darted into their holes and others that were further away popped up. They stayed a safe distance from the humans but still kept tabs on us. As the light faded, they all disappeared beneath the surface; it was time to call it a day.

Prairie Dog

The tourists were vanishing too, as they returned to their campsites or hotels. We drove further and then pulled off the road and stopped the car. We gathered flashlights and blankets and walked a short distance into the craggy landscape. We had brought my large Taos drum, so we didn't go far from the car.

We spread the blankets and set the drum in the center. I looked around at the surroundings, and it reminded me of videos I had seen taken on the moon. The surface was rocky and devoid of color. It seemed strange to be sitting on what looked like the moon and also see the moon in the sky.

LuAnn, however, was not seeing the beauty in being there. No sooner had we spread the blankets than she wanted to return to the tent. We tried to convince her she was safe, assuring her we wouldn't stay long. We smudged ourselves and the drum with the sweet sage I had previously gathered and set our intention for the evening, but we had no way of knowing the gift we were about to receive.

Taos Drum

I started a rhythmic beat on the drum and stopped after a few minutes. In the distance, coyotes began howling. They stopped, so Alexandria took up the beat. She stopped, and again the coyotes replied. We continued this *dialog* with the same results. It was exciting and fun to be talking with these wild creatures. Unfortunately, LuAnn did not agree. It scared her and she wanted to go back to camp, so sadly, we left. We went back to camp and crawled into our beds. The coyotes had made it an evening to remember.

Singing Coyote

The next morning, when we popped out of our tents, there were four buffaloes grazing on the few blades of grass that grew in the campground. Their presence was marked by the *buffalo pies* (dung) that littered the area. Buffaloes can be dangerous, but they were just having breakfast and had no interest in humans. Rarely do they attack unless people are doing something that threatens them or their calves.

Buffalo Grazing

A trip to the outhouse revealed there were also a few horses in the park. Their trailers were parked, the cowboys were having coffee and laughing, and the animals were tied to the hitching rail munching hay that their owners had brought with them. We hadn't seen them, so they must have come while we were out with the coyotes or during the night.

After a camp breakfast, we discussed what we were going to do next. It was a beautiful day and there was much more to explore, but LuAnn had had enough of nature; it was time to go back to the city.

The Takeaway: When we get beyond our fears, nature often gives us gifts we never expected.

Story 29
The Tetons

No book of camping stories would be complete without a bear story. I have encountered them a few times on the trails; this one was cool, not scary.

In the 1990s, a lady I met in the Bahamas was going to lead a retreat in Teton National Park, Wyoming, and she invited me to join them. When the day arrived, I drove to the Tetons from western South Dakota where I was living. The retreat provided magical experiences with the other attendees and the mountains, and I knew I had to return. Twenty years later, I would keep that promise to myself.

It was late summer and I was on a walk-about through western Wyoming. Most of the tourists had already left the area, but I didn't know how crowded the Teton National Park would be, so I stopped at a primitive campground just outside the park. The area felt deserted, despite the two RVs parked there. There were no human noises, not even generators. The squirrels and the breeze in the trees were the only sounds I heard. It was kind of eerie.

I pitched my tent anyway and made my bed. It would get chilly, so I made sure I had my hat, slipper socks, and enough blankets to stay warm. I had found that having my head and feet warm went a long way toward keeping my body temperature at a comfortable level. When I went to bed, I would place my coat nearby to throw over my head, which would hold in my body heat and still allow me to breathe easily. Of course, my four-inch foam mat would help keep me warm and off the ground. I would be quite comfortable.

Bear Warning Sign

There were warning signs for bears on the road and in the campground. Sleeping in a tent in an isolated area designated as *bear country* had me a bit concerned, but I told myself it would be okay. I wasn't sure I believed it, but I was here and planned to stay the night. I had a simple dinner and put everything I didn't need for the night in the car. Bears have a keen sense of smell, so I carefully sealed food in containers and put them in the ice chest which then went into the car trunk. I hoped that would diminish any odors and not attract unwanted guests.

I sat for a while sipping tea and peering into the forest. The wind came up, and it cooled off quickly, so I retreated to my tent. I curled up, happy that I had a soft, warm bed. It had been a long day on the road, and I was ready to rest. I listened to the wind blowing through the treetops and soon fell asleep.

During the night, I was startled awake; something had hit my tent! I lay waiting. My senses were on high alert when something else hit the tent. I told myself it was a pine cone falling from the tree overhead. But was it? I waited a bit longer and nothing came crashing through my tent, so I reassured myself that it was just a pine cone and went back to sleep.

Despite the scare, I slept well. When I got up the next morning, I was eager to go hiking in the national forest. I drove into the park, and knowing it was first come first served, I found a camping space for that night. After paying the fee, I set up camp.

The park has bear boxes, which are food storage lockers big enough to accommodate ice chests. They keep the critters from raiding peoples' camps, and hopefully, deter the bears from coming into the campground. I put my cooler in the box and left my site.

I studied the map of the hiking areas to see if I could find the route we had hiked when I was there years before, but none seemed familiar. One seemed more likely than the others so I drove to that trailhead. I parked my car in the lot, got my backpack out of the trunk, and stuffed it with a blanket, my journal, snacks, and a few other necessities. I stopped in the restroom, and while washing my hands, dropped my water bottle. After picking it up and cleaning it off, I set out on a marked trail. Many people were making the same journey, so safety seemed assured despite the signs. "Safety in numbers" and all that.

I stopped a few times on the trail to absorb my surroundings. At one point, I saw a bear up a slight incline on my left sitting in some brush. It was a berry patch, and he was stuffing his face with berries. He was so busy feasting that he paid no attention to the hikers.

Bears on Trails Warning Sign

Further down the path, we all stopped in our tracks when a black bear dropped from a branch 20 feet off the ground, then another and another. We all stared in quiet amazement. It was a mom and her two cubs. Mom stood up, shook herself, and the family wandered off into the woods as if nothing had happened. They were seemingly unaware of the people watching a few feet from them.

Bears falling from Tree

After walking a long way and not finding the area I wanted to revisit, I stopped for a drink of water. The bottle was less than half full, and I had only had one drink from it. Unfortunately, when I dropped the bottle, it cracked slightly, and the water had been leaking out. Not having a full bottle was not good, as I had a long walk back.

One thing I keep in mind when hiking is to only walk half as far as I think I can because I have to retrace my steps back to my starting point. On this hike, I wasn't thinking about that. I was focused on the bears and my surroundings, and searching for things that would confirm I was on the trail I wanted. Nothing stood out.

Disappointed that this was not the right trail and with so little water left, I decided it was time to turn back. Why had I gone so far? My back was aching, and every step I took was an effort. I had to stop several times, and part of me was wishing a bear would attack me, so the rangers would carry me out on a stretcher. The pain grew, but there was no choice; I had to push through it and keep going.

I eventually made it to the car, and in great relief, tumbled into the driver's seat. I was sad I had not found the trail I wanted and also elated to have experienced the bears so close up. Despite my thoughts on the trail, I was grateful I did not get mauled or eaten. It is funny what the mind comes up with when one is stressed or in pain!

I drove back to my campsite. As I slowly crept through the campground, I saw bears at several sites. They were chomping handfuls of bread and food the people had left on their picnic tables. Why hadn't they used the bear boxes? One family was excitedly taking pictures of the bears as they fed them their chips. These bears could become a real menace to campers, and then the Rangers would have to take action. That is sad for everyone.

So much for the bear boxes and warning signs!

The Takeaway: Wild animals are awesome to watch, but respecting the fact that they are wild can prevent injuries.

Story 30
Spiritual Woodstock

The owners of Canyon Calm, 10 miles outside of Custer, South Dakota, were hosting a Spiritual Woodstock event over the 2013 summer solstice.

I had missed the 1969 Woodstock. In '69, my life revolved around my young children and I knew nothing about those things. I didn't even know there was a Woodstock until my daughter mentioned it when she was a teenager. Boy, was I out of it! So when I heard about the Spiritual Woodstock gathering, I went online and did more research. This event sounded promising since the focus was on celebrating Native American traditions, and no mention was made of drugs. (It turned out there were both.)

The facility was on 40 acres and we were welcome to bring motorhomes, vans, or tents for camping. There was an area where attendees could set up booths to sell their products and do intuitive readings, reflexology, or chair massages—whatever area of expertise they wanted to share. There were also places for circles, a sweat lodge, tipi, fires, and other activities.

There was a schedule outlined on the website. Each day would start with yoga. Then there were children's activities, talks, circles, a sweat lodge, and ceremonies loosely organized throughout the weekend. Meals were mostly on our own, but a community meal was served each day. The days ended with live music from a different band each evening.

My friend Michael, his wife, and their boys met me there. They were from Denver and Michael was excited to introduce his family to camping. He had purchased the latest in camping equipment to make it an enjoyable experience for them. As soon as he got their camp set up, his wife said she was getting sunburned and didn't want to stay. So he drove her and the children to a hotel in Custer that had a swimming pool. That was where they happily spent the weekend. Michael was disappointed, but at least, he had my friend Alexandria and me to hang out with. We pitched our tents close to one another so we could walk back together from the evening campfire.

When we finished making camp, Alexandria and I went to the gathering area and erected a canopy in which to do Reiki. We had a few people stop by, but most people focused on the sweat lodge, playing with the children, doing crafts, and participating in circles and ceremonies. In the end, this worked out well for us, as it allowed us to visit with people, take part in some events, and hike. Michael spent his days in town with his family and then came back for the evening.

Activities continued throughout the day and into the night. The communal meal was served at lunchtime. It was delicious and had something for everyone, no matter what one's food preferences were. My friends and I ate at the long tables that were set up for meals and also used for creative art projects.

At night, there was a small fire circle and also a bigger one that accommodated the entire group. After a ceremony at the large circle, people congregated in small groups around both fires to talk more intimately. The small ring had a 12-inch high stone circle around the pit, and besides keeping the fire contained, it gave me a resting place for my feet.

I sat in my folding chair with my feet propped on the rocks. As I sat there staring into the fire, I noticed steam coming up from my shoes and thought that was strange, until I realized the soles on my shoes were melting from the extreme heat! I did a swift dance in the dirt and extinguished the smoldering rubber.

On the last day of the event, the wind blew with gale-force strength. We had to get the canopy down and packed in its bag. We got it down, but there was no way to fold it while the wind was trying to take it away, and us with it. We threw it in the car; I would have to take care of that once I got home.

After Alexandria and I got ours down, I sat my snack bag on the ground behind the car, thinking I would put it in the trunk once we helped Don with his tarp. When we finished, we all jumped in our cars to get out of the pelting sand. Unfortunately, I forgot about my bag in the back of the car and drove over it. There was a loud explosion as my glass-lined vacuum thermos blew up. People came running to see what had happened, and we all had a good laugh. I didn't know a thermos did that, but I do now!

There was no point in hanging around with the fierce wind; it was time to leave. A friend was going to follow me to the highway, but unfortunately, someone had given her an *edible* before we left. After driving a few miles, I looked back, and she was nowhere to be seen. I waited for a long time, and eventually, she came up behind me smiling and driving 5 mph. She had gotten engrossed in how beautiful the scenery was and lost track of time and where she was. That must have been a good brownie!

This weekend was pleasant enough, and I assumed the 1969 event was similar, so I left feeling I may not have gotten my Woodstock experience in *the* '60s, instead, I got it in *my* 60s.

The Takeaway: You never know what will happen at an event called Woodstock.

Story 31
Dinner Woes and Sweetness

As I was lighting the camp stove to prepare dinner, my mind drifted from Ajo to a long-past camping trip in Colorado. On that trip, I learned much about camp stoves, and it was after that adventure that I found a foolproof one. As I recounted that weekend in my mind, I also had to smile at the differences between camping in the desert and camping in the mountains.

My daughter, grandson, and I were living in Boulder, Colorado. We chose a weekend to go camping and drove into the Colorado Rockies. As we drove, it was drizzling rain. The sun was trying to show itself when we arrived at the campsite, but it was not doing a very good job. It was chilly and damp. We had the weekend to enjoy the fresh forest air and babbling stream, and we were not going to let the weather ruin our outing. Besides, as they say in Colorado, "If you don't like the weather, wait five minutes and it will change."

We set up our tents. I put mine by the creek, as I wanted to hear the running water. Jodi placed theirs away from the stream, which turned out to be the wiser choice because by the time we began preparing dinner, the stream was no longer a babbling brook but more of a raging river due to the rain runoff. Not knowing if it would overflow its banks in the night, I dragged my tent a safe distance from the water.

After we got things organized in camp, it was time to play. Brandon, my eight-year-old grandson, loved when he and I laid trails and his mom followed them. We took sticks and rocks and put them at intervals through the forest, pointing in the direction she should go to reach the next marker. When we finished, we called her to the starting line and watched as she tried to find her way. We were good at our job, so it was easy for her to follow the trail we had made, but she would pretend she was lost. He squealed with delight. It was a fun game we played, and it kept him entertained much longer than it did me.

Some of the Trail Markers We Used

When it started drizzling again, we decided we had better prepare dinner. My dad had lent us his two-burner stove, and I had bought a propane fuel canister for it. I thought it would be more useful because my pump-up stove had only one burner, but when we opened Dad's, there was no hose to connect it to the fuel. We would not be cooking on that stove. Knowing my dad as I did, I should have checked it before we left home.

As a backup, I had brought my one-burner pump-up. Its burner and the fuel tank were one piece, so there was no hose. I liked the pump-up gas version because it worked better at high altitudes than the propane stove. The drawback was that it was harder to use since it had to be pumped and adjusted, but I had used it many times and had become a pro at getting it to work. I pumped it up, and we started cooking the chicken. While it was sizzling, the flame went out and it would not start again. I checked the fuel, and it was still almost full; that was not the problem.

My pump-up had never failed me. Later, I took it to a dealer, and he sold me a part that extended its life. While I was in his store, I bought a one-burner that screwed directly onto the butane fuel tank, and that has worked well for years. The only drawback is that it is not as stable as the other models.

Camp Stoves

We gathered kindling, and with lots of newspaper and lighter fluid, started a fire, but the wood was damp and it never got hot; it just smoked a lot. So that would not cook our dinner. With two stoves down and no dry firewood, it was time to move on to the charcoal. We had only planned to cook s'mores on it if there was no firewood, so there wasn't much in the bag. We used what was there to finish cooking the chicken. Amazingly, it did get done. Because of the weather, there would be no sitting around any kind of fire with s'mores anyway.

Wet Smoldering Fire

It took two hours to prepare the meal, and it was still spitting rain when we finished. It had been a challenge, and we were happy at the thought of sitting

212

down in the tent where it was dry and enjoying the dinner that had been such a challenge to prepare. What we saw when we entered the tent brought tears to my eyes!

While Jodi and I had been using all means to cook dinner, Brandon had been preparing a *table* for us in the tent. He had spread a towel out and arranged the plates, tableware, and glasses on it. Salt and pepper were in the center next to the wildflowers and pinecones he had gathered for the centerpiece. He placed pillows around it for us to sit on. The creativity and kindness of this eight-year-old child made the craziness of the last few hours fade. It lifted our spirits, put a smile on our faces, and turned it into a special event. His loving, kind act was an experience I have treasured.

Brandon's Table

It was dark when we finished eating. I stepped out of their tent and looked upward. It had stopped raining, but the sky was still heavy with clouds and no stars were visible. I put the dirty plates and leftovers in the park dumpster, just in case there were hungry bears in the area. I took one last look around and went into my tent, where my bed was waiting for me.

It felt good to climb into my dry, warm covers after the wet, unpredictable day we had experienced. I lay there thinking about how my grandson had changed the dismal hours spent preparing the meal into a joyous feast. I smiled and slept.

The Takeaway: Simplify meals. Check your equipment. Let your family know how special they are.

Story 32
The Invisibles

Before I left on my trip to Ajo, I packed a small lamp for reading in the evening. I chose a lamp because I prefer the soft incandescent light they provide to that of a lantern. I wrapped the lightbulb in a hand towel and put it under the front seat, figuring that was the safest place to keep it from getting broken and it would be easy to find.

When I arrived at my campsite, I set up the tent and took my accessories inside. I had the lamp, but when I looked under the seat for the bulb, it was not there. That was strange. I continued to look and did not find it, but no worries. There was a dollar store close by, and later I would walk over and purchase another one.

Dollar stores are of great benefit to folks in towns too small to host a Target or Walmart. They have a bit of everything, are reasonably priced, and the checkout lines are never long. People still have to go to the city for major shopping, but for odds and ends, they are indeed a blessing. I was pleased there was one close by.

The Lightbulb

By the time I had camp organized and my dinner was eaten, the sun had dipped behind the hill and the air began to cool. It was time to walk to the store, so I went to the car to get my wallet. I opened the car door and there, lying on the backseat in plain sight, was the lightbulb! I was flabbergasted. How did it get there and where had it been? I had not put it there, yet there it was. Confused, I picked it up and marveled at the mystery.

An interesting thing is that much later in my trip, I was at my grandson's house and one of his lightbulbs burned out. I just happened to have one under my seat! When we went to my car and I pulled it out and handed it to him, he just looked at me and shook his head.

As I thought about this, I remembered this was not the first time I had things vanish and then reappear. It was just one more occurrence of high strangeness that my brain still hasn't worked out.

Another mysterious disappearance occurred after one of my camping trips. Before I left town for the mountains, I went to the bank and withdrew a sizable amount of cash. I would be in areas where there were no banks, and I didn't know if I could use a credit card. I wanted to make sure I had enough money for anything that arose.

I completed my travels and drove to Denver to visit a friend. I got my things out of the car, and oddly, the money was not there. Multiple times, I searched my pockets, purse, suitcase, and car. My friend helped me look, but it was nowhere to be found. I was distraught, as there was a substantial amount of cash left in the envelope, but there was nothing more to be done. I accepted the fact that it would either turn up or it was gone.

The next morning, I went to the car to take another look. I was stunned to see the bank envelope lying on the backseat. It was there in full view, not the least bit hidden. I knew it had not been there the previous day. I counted the money, and it was all there. My relief overrode the questions that sprang to mind, like where had it been, and how did it get there? I didn't know the answers but gratefully accepted its return.

As if these two events weren't strange enough, there was another disappearance that occurred while camping in the Bighorn Mountains. I was loading the car, preparing to leave after a few days in the forest, and could not find my car keys. I remembered unlocking the car door and placing them on the picnic table, yet when I went to get them to open the trunk, they were not there.

Some fellow campers were walking by and stopped to visit. I related my story, and they walked around my campsite, helping me look for them. The keys did not show up, and I could only assume that a bird, squirrel, or some mischievous character had carried them off to its nest.

The Key Thief?

I always carry a spare electronic key for just such an emergency. Knowing I had the backup helped calm my anxiety. Here in the mountains, there were no tow trucks or locksmiths close by. The closest services were an hour away in Buffalo, Wyoming, but there would have been no way to call them since phone service was non-existent. It would cost me $200 to replace the key, but at that moment, it seemed like a small price to pay not to have the problems I could have encountered.

I finished loading the car and made one final circle of my campsite, checking to see if I missed anything. I was happy I made that last check because there on the picnic table lay my ring of keys! They were right where I had left them.

My $200 Key on Picnic Table

I was relieved to find them, but where had they been? Did the squirrel or bird return them? I doubted it and chalked it up to another unsolved mystery. Disappearing and reappearing lightbulb, money, and keys? How did this happen? I had no explanation, and no, I am not that absent-minded.

All I can say is that I had crossed over into some misty region of *The Twilight Zone.*

The Takeaway: Stay out of the Twilight Zone!

Story 33
I Found It or Did It Find Me?

While I was on my nine-month walk-about, I drove over 15,000 miles. Part of that summer, I spent in South Dakota working in my nephew's wood shop. He has a building and tool for every job, including a sawmill, kiln, sanding area, finishing area, showroom, and wood storage barn. He taught me how to load the kiln and to use the saws, sanders, and planers.

Saw Mill and Cut Wood

I helped him and was also free to work on my projects. This was more physical labor than I was used to, and my body fell into bed at night. It was worth the discomfort because it was magical working with wood and sharing the company of my nephew.

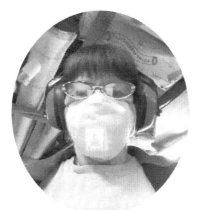

My Shop Girl Selfie

Following through on my idea to purchase a house in Ajo for a winter residence, I used my downtime to research homes that were for sale in Ajo, Arizona. I also looked at financing options. Once I found the best arrangements for me, I filled out the paperwork. Being pre-qualified let me know my price point, and I narrowed my search to homes in that range. I found a few online and was eager to go inside them.

It was sad leaving my nephew, but we had accomplished much while I was there, and it was time to continue my search. I began my drive back to Ajo, but I did not hurry as it would still be hot there.

When I arrived in Ajo, it was mid-September, and I found that summer still had not left the desert. It was 98 degrees during the day. It cooled to 75 degrees by 11:00 p.m., but the night didn't last very long and the temperature chased me from my tent by 6:00 a.m. I had brought a fan with me, so I could circulate the air in my tent at night, but once the sun rose, the tent became an oven.

The RVers were not as naïve as me about the weather in the Southwest, so they had not yet returned and the park was virtually empty. The only people there were the ones that had permanent trailers with air conditioning. They mostly ignored me, even when I waved or said hello.

Trees were few in the park, so during my travels, I purchased an awning at a garage sale and attempted to set it up so I would have shade. Staying out of the scorching desert sun makes a vast difference in temperature and comfort. The awning was a challenge to set up because it kept falling apart. I'd get the pipes connected in one place, and it fell apart in another. I taped it hoping that would hold it till I got it together, but that wasn't the best solution; I needed another pair of hands. After a few hours of struggling, I finally got it put together. Then I staked it. It took a lot of effort, but it was up. However, I had little confidence that it would stay.

Unlike the winter campers who cheerfully offered help and encouragement, the permanent residents watched from behind curtains and sunscreens as I struggled. No help or encouragement was forthcoming. Later, I learned they were not only watching, but they were laughing at my plight. It was a very different experience than I had with the snowbirds earlier that year.

I left my site to go to the market for some supplies, and when I returned, the awning was twisted and flopping like a fish out of water. The ground was so hard that I could not get the stakes securely anchored. I untangled it and set it right. I went to bed, not sure what I would find in the morning.

During the night, I could hear the fabric flapping in the wind. I wanted the shade it provided, but in the morning when it was in a heap on the ground, it was time to admit defeat. I took what remained standing down, but I couldn't get it apart because the metal pieces had bent and were now stuck together. In frustration, I gathered up all the pieces and carried them to the dumpster. Enough already!

When I drove past the dumpster later that day, it was gone, so someone who knew about these things took it, and I am sure it served the new owner well.

Since I had no shade at my campsite, I had to find places to spend the day out of the sun. The town's library and the RV park's clubhouse served this purpose for a few hours each day. I also spent time in the realtor's office or driving around in my air-conditioned car looking at houses. Never have I been that grateful for air conditioning!

Considering the size of the town, there were a surprising number of homes for sale in my price range. After I chose a few houses, the realtor drove me to see the inside of them. Most of the homes were built quickly as housing for the miners in the 1950s, so they were old and not well-constructed. They needed repairs that were bigger projects than I wanted to tackle.

A Typical House in Ajo, AZ

After searching, I found a house I liked that had been renovated. I stopped at the RV park's office and talked to the manager about it and her life in Ajo. While I was there, the man from the trailer next to my camp space came in to pick up his mail. Once introduced, he talked freely. After telling me how he and his wife had laughed at me trying to set up the canopy, he was a wealth of information about the homes, as he was a repairman in town.

I told him about the house I found; it seemed nearly perfect, and it was stylishly updated. He gave me questions to ask the realtor to find out if they had performed more than cosmetic work. They had replaced the electrical box, but what about the rest of the wiring? The plumbing in the house had been replaced, but had the sewer line to the street? He said these things were failing in many houses. There was no landscaping, and it would require equipment to work the rocky soil as a shovel would not penetrate it. After attempting to get tent stakes into the ground, I did not doubt that. These would all be costly projects and the workers would

224

have to come from Phoenix since I doubted his integrity to do the work.

I did not want to contact the realtor to ask my questions, as she had not been forthcoming about other things I asked. There were few legal documents, and what was there was of no help. As I looked for answers, I saw the bad feelings between the realtors and also between other people in town. There were underlying currents of animosity that I did not want to be part of. This town of 3,000 people was small, and I was not sure how one could become part of a community that was divided without getting involved in their issues.

In the end, I contacted a different realtor with the questions he presented and found that the really expensive projects had not been done. Since this was the best of the houses I had toured, I went back to my tent to reevaluate purchasing a home in the desert where water could also become an issue.

Disappointed, I asked myself if I truly wanted to deal with the unexpected expenses that could come with a house, especially in an area where workers and supplies had to come 115 miles from Phoenix to do the work. Was I a renter at heart?

The following is a journal entry dated September 22, 2019.

I am wondering if the life I have imagined is that of a younger me. Do I want to work this hard at this point in my life? I made it through yesterday, although I was verging on heatstroke. The sweat leeched minerals from my body, and my feet and legs cramped during the night.

It is now 6:30 in the morning and it is lovely, but that will change soon. The birds are singing; the breeze is blowing, and in the shade it is comfortable, but if yesterday is any sign of what the temperatures will be later in the day, it means another 100-degree day with 44 percent humidity. To people who live here, that is probably okay but for someone from South Dakota, it is next to torture.

I spent much of the day lying on the couch in the clubhouse icing my ankles because they were swollen from the heat. This place is truly hotter than hell during the day, even this late in the year. My body can't tolerate it. Many houses do not have adequate heating and cooling, and living here without air conditioning is no more feasible than living without heat in South Dakota.

I was looking forward to buying a house here and making it my own, but that involves either a lot of money or energy. Just getting the canopy up was a challenge; I did it, but there were lots of expletives. The fact that workers and building materials have to come from Phoenix complicates things even further. I do not want to always be trying to find a reliable person to help me or be pouring my money into fixing a house.

Last winter, I had my dream for a life in Ajo crushed when Curley School didn't work. Now I'm back for another go at it, and I have gotten another reality check. No matter what I try, it doesn't work. My conclusion is, "I don't belong here." As they say, "It is like chewing gum, and all the flavor is gone out of it."

The desert was an outstanding place to rest and rejuvenate, and even spend the winter, but when I am being realistic, I see that living here and owning a home is

226

not the reality I want to live in. It took me nine months on the road to realize this. Now what?

I'm back to wanting answers and yet having no plan. I am open; I have been patient for nine months and now I just want to know. The details of the future are not important, as long as it feeds my heart and soul.

What do I truly want? I want to feel joy every day, be energized by my surroundings, have kind people around me, and live in a gentle climate. (The list of how I wanted my life to feel continued.) I don't care where I live, but Santa Fe has many things I like in a community. As I feel into what my life there can be, joy fills me. Again, I relax and stop worrying or questioning. Instead, I go into my quiet space and feel joy for no reason.

Written later in the day:

While I was in my joy space this morning, the phone rang. It was the senior apartment complex in Santa Fe that I had applied to three years earlier! I emailed them in March to check my place on the availability list, and now six months later, I am hearing from them. They have an apartment and it is mine if I want it. Do I want it? You betcha!

I am overjoyed! Life is sweeter in Santa Fe with Trader Joe's, Sprouts, the arts, my friends, an airport close by, pleasant weather most days, and the smell of chilis roasting in the fall. I have always liked Santa Fe and am so ready for this to be my home. Right now, I appreciate the thought of it more than ever.

I needed the experiences of the last nine months to truly appreciate this opportunity. So much happened on my walkabout, and I probably wasn't ready three years ago when I applied, or even nine months ago when I began this journey. I am now!

Outdoor Chile Roasting, Santa Fe

If you remember in Story 1, *The Plan*, I was reading the rental ads for Santa Fe. That was where I wanted to live. Curley School in Ajo came up in the list of ads, and with all the artists who lived there, it sounded like a fun place to be. Being surrounded by artists and avoiding the high rental prices in Santa Fe inspired me to apply to Curley.

I thought that was a synchronicity to get me to Ajo. I suppose it was synchronistic, but not for the reason I thought. It took me on a drive-about that brought so many experiences I wouldn't have had otherwise, all of which took me full circle back to living in Santa Fe.

At present, I live in Santa Fe. I am a renter and love my home. I am happy and feel blessed to be here.

The Takeaway: Follow your heart and don't worry about a Plan. Things will all come together when the time is right.

AND SHE
LIVED
HAPPILY EVER
AFTER

About the Author

Nancy DeYoung

As a child growing up in eastern South Dakota, Nancy DeYoung found comfort in her makeshift tents, but it wasn't until she had her own children that she grew to love camping. Her family of five often spent weekends at the lake boating and camping.

After the children were grown and her husband was no longer part of the picture, Nancy continued her travels and outdoor adventures to numerous countries and throughout the U.S. She now lives in Santa Fe, New Mexico, which she calls her "forever home."

Ms. DeYoung is also the author of *Modern Shamans* and *Shaman's Vision*.

To Order Books

Modern Shamans, Shaman's Vision, and *the Girl in the Tent* are available in, or can be ordered from, most book-stores. They can also be purchased online from Amazon.com.

Modern Shamans is an instructional manual on emotional clearing. It provides information and simple, effective exercises that help clear the emotional charge connected to our memories. By doing this, we are no longer triggered by things people say and do. We are freed from the repetitious cycles and patterns in which we have been living. We find that the way forward in life is to go within our Selves where wholeness, understanding, and direction await us. This is the journey of the modern shaman!
9780615142227, 196 pages, 6x9, paperback

Shaman's Vision calls us to wake up and snap out of the hypnotically controlled state we may not even know we live under. With information and practice, we can become *modern shamans*. From this state, we learn to see subtle energies and how they affect us. We see the patterns and programs that influence our lives. We also see how to step out of them so we can live in expanded truth. To understand the unseen forces that may be working in your life, you will want to read this book today!
9780984410330, 208 pages, 6x9, paperback